Stylish SweatJackets

Fran Morgan

Located in Paducah, Kentucky, the American Quilter's Society (AQS) is dedicated to promoting the accomplishments of today's quilters. Through its publications and events, AQS strives to honor today's quiltmakers and their work and to inspire future creativity and innovation in quiltmaking.

Executive Editor: Andi Milam Reynolds
Senior Editor: Linda Baxter Lasco
Technical Editor: Marcelle Cashon
Graphic Design: Elaine Wilson
Cover Design: Michael Buckingham
Photography: Charles R. Lynch

Special thanks to models: Amberly Craig, Jessica Kravchak, Courtney Mitchell, baby Maxson, and Mister Beasley

Additional copies of this book may be ordered from the American Quilter's Society, PO Box 3290, Paducah, KY 42002-3290, or online at www.AmericanQuilter.com.

Library of Congress Cataloging-in-Publication Data

Morgan, Fran.
Stylish sweatjackets / by Fran Morgan.
p. cm.
ISBN 978-1-57432-995-7
1. Jackets. 2. Clothing and dress--Remaking. I. Title.
TT535.M67 2009
646.4'57--dc22

2009020733

Acknowledgments

I would like to thank the following people for their continued help and support while I was putting this book together:

My business partner and mother, Donna, for being willing to answer the question, no matter how many times it was asked, "Does this look okay?" Also, for her continued enthusiasm for my designing and her amazing talents in sales and marketing!

For my husband, Mel, who holds me up at the end of a long, tough day, who is forever patient with my crazy ideas, and who lets me sew and quilt when I want to, even when he's hungry. Without Mel's support, none of this could be possible for me.

A Special Thank You

I would like to thank the following companies for donating products for this book. I couldn't have done it without you!

Benartex for their beautiful fabrics
Ghee's for zippers and organza
Collins for the Wash Away Wonder™ Tape
Fabric Café for sweatshirts and Chenille By The Inch® strips

Contents

Basic Instructions

Before You Begin

If you have never taken a sweatshirt and turned it into a jacket, it can be a daunting task. Most of us love the idea, but have had little success in creating a jacket we can be proud of. In this book I hope to alleviate your fears, step you through a few little tricks, and help you create a stunning jacket tailored just for you.

First, you're on the right track. You are reading through the Basic Instructions. Many of the things you will need to know for a great finished jacket are in this first section. Each of the patterns in this book will refer back to instructions and illustrations in this section. Don't forget to review the Basic Supplies list (page 9). These supplies will be extremely helpful for achieving a great finished look. As always, the right tools make the job easier.

Once you have chosen a pattern you would like to make, review the Materials list. Supplies specific to the pattern will be listed there. Fabric colors, amounts, and a list of cutting measurements will be next in the Fabric Requirements and Cutting Instructions. Before you begin with step 1 of the pattern, cut all fabric pieces as listed for each fabric. I often use the abbreviation "WOF," which means "width of fabric." For example, if the required measurement is 1½" x WOF, you would cut a strip of fabric 1½" wide from selvage to selvage.

If the fabric measurements include a bias cut, cut the bias strips first, then cut the remaining pieces. Bias strips are essential in most sweatshirt neck edges because you must have a bias strip to finish the curved edge neatly without bunching or puckering. Cutting bias can be scary for some, but is actually very easy to do. You will need a long ruler (I prefer a 24" ruler) that has a 45-degree angle line. Place the 45-degree line on the selvage of the fabric and cut along the ruler's edge (fig. 1). Make subsequent cuts along the bias-cut edge in the width indicated in your pattern.

Once the fabric pieces are cut, it's time to start making the jacket. I use a ¼" seam allowance throughout. If the seam allowance is different, it will be stated in the pattern. Because I use a ¼" seam so often, I love my ¼" presser foot. For me it's a necessity for making sweatshirt jackets—sweatjackets. There are several other presser feet I use from time to time, so please double-check the pattern Materials lists for these.

To assist you in making each jacket, there are illustrations showing some of the steps.

Selecting a Pattern

Pattern selection is as critical to a fabulous fit as is your workmanship and the quality of your supplies. I have included several different styles in this book to address different fit issues, but first let me address some basic tricks to help you choose.

When designing a sweatjacket, I always create a vertical line instead of a horizontal line. Therefore, I turn my hem facings under so they don't show. A horizontal line falling right on my hip gives the illusion that I'm wider than I really am. However, if I create a vertical line down the center front, my height is emphasized.

The only exception to this rule is when the focus is on the waistline. For instance, the CINCHED WAIST JACKET and the DRAWSTRING JACKET both have horizontal lines at the waist. This draws the eye away from hips and thighs directly to the waist, creating an hour-glass figure.

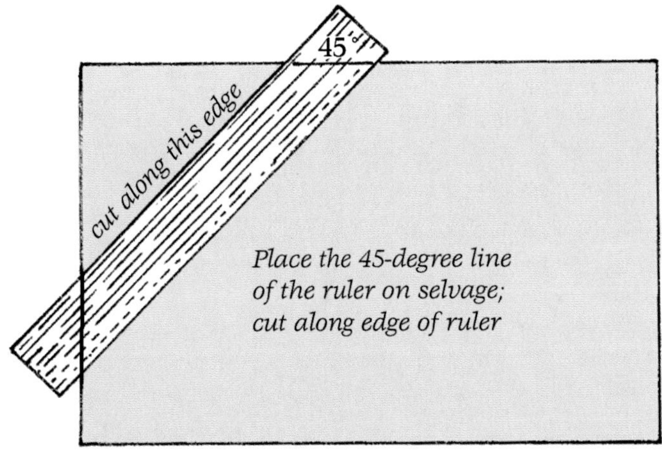

FIG. 1. Cutting bias

A sloped or narrow shoulder is a tricky fit issue. The Swing Jacket with Shoulder Pleats is an excellent way to bring in the shoulder and still have a great fit everywhere else. The shoulder pleats bring the shoulder seam up creating a better fit for a sloped or narrow shoulder. Experiment with these pleats. They can be used on any of these patterns. Just remember to sew them in before trimming the sleeve length.

There are lots of great finishing touches on these sweatjackets. Feel free to mix and match your favorite elements. If you love the Long Tunic, but would prefer it with shoulder pleats, you certainly can do that. Just follow the pleat directions from the Swing Jacket with Shoulder Pleats, then continue with the instructions for the Long Tunic. If you prefer a V-neck instead of a round neck, just follow the instructions for cutting and finishing a V-neck from the Cinched Waist or Ruffled Jacket pattern.

Choosing a Sweatshirt

The sweatshirt you choose when making a sweatjacket is the "bones" of your project. If the bones are strong, so is the finished project. If you would like to use the same sweatshirts that I use, check out the Resources (page 77).

Here is what to consider when purchasing a sweatshirt to refashion into a sweatjacket.

First, the fiber content is important. I recommend 80 percent cotton and 20 percent polyester. I prefer this blend because the high cotton content presses crisply and finishes with a clean edge, while the 20 percent polyester keeps the cotton from stretching out of shape when I wear it. The polyester also helps to keep the shape of the jacket when it is washed.

Second, purchase the size sweatshirt that you normally wear. Do not go a size bigger. Our goal is to make a nicely fitting jacket that is not too slouchy or big. Sweatshirt manufacturers include a lot of extra ease in the sizing because normally sweatshirts are worn for active wear or over another shirt, so they require extra room for movement. Here we are aiming for a more tailored look, which does not require as much ease. If you find that you are between sizes, choose the larger of the two. Don't forget to check if the sweatshirt is preshrunk. If there is a high cotton content and it is not preshrunk, allow for shrinkage. This means you may need to choose a size larger. Always prewash the sweatshirt before beginning your project.

Third, look for a sweatshirt without side seams. I learned this one day when I bought a beautifully colored sweatshirt to make into a jacket. When I cut off the bottom band, to my surprise the side seams twisted. I tried and tried to find a way to make a jacket from this sweatshirt, but no matter what, those side seams would be obviously twisted.

Finally, give the sweatshirt the once-over. Make sure there is no variation of color, no flaws in the fabric, nor holes; I've actually bought a sweatshirt and later discovered a small hole. Check the sleeve depth by folding the sweatshirt in half, matching shoulder and underarm seams. Are the sleeves the same distance from shoulder seam to underarm? Is it the same distance from neckband to shoulder seam on both sides? If either of these measurements is off, your jacket will be off-center and not fit properly.

Basic Supplies

Following is a list of basic supplies you will need to finish your sweatjacket. I've included a brief description of how some of the items will be used.

* **Thread to match fabrics**
* **Hand sewing needle**
* **Scissors**—for snipping threads and removing the bands at the bottom and sleeves.
* **Rotary cutter**—for trimming the sweatshirt edges so your jacket hangs perfectly.
* **24" or longer quilt ruler**—It's best when your ruler is as long as your sweatshirt from hem to neck edge.
* **Large self-healing cutting mat with grid lines**—for cutting fabrics and the sweatshirt.
* **Small self-healing cutting mat with grid lines**—to slip inside the sweatshirt when cutting the front open
* **Chalk marker, or other fabric marking tool, in white and blue**—to mark front openings, sleeve length, sides, and other fabric placements. Blue is best for light colored sweatshirts; white is best for dark colored sweatshirts.
* **Seam ripper**—for removing neck bands.
* **Spray starch or other spray stabilizer**—to stabilize raw edges of sweatshirt before sewing; it helps give a crisp press.
* **Straight pins**
* **¼" presser foot**—makes sewing easy and fast since most of the seam allowances are ¼".
* **Edge stitch presser foot**—there is a lot of edge/top stitching in sweatshirt refashioning; this foot helps keep stitching straight and perfectly on the edge.
* **¼" water-soluble basting tape**—I highly recommend this product when working with sweatshirts. The tape is ¼" wide, water-soluble, and won't gum up your needle.

Using Water-soluble Tape

I use this tape to turn under ¼" edges. A ¼" edge is tough to press under straight, so the tape is a way that I "cheat" to get the perfect ¼" turn under.

* Place the tape on the wrong side of the fabric, along the entire raw edge needing to be turned ¼".
* With a dry iron (can be finger pressed), fold the fabric under and press, using the paper on the tape to give a ridged edge to press against.
* Remove the paper from the tape and stick the edge in place along the pressed edge.

The tape is also great as a straight pin replacement, especially when putting in the pleats. The tape holds the pleats in place so you can put the jacket on and check the placement before sewing. If the placement looks good, I can stitch it down, no straight pins needed. Sweatshirt fleece can be thick when folded. The tape keeps the fleece smooth and straight where a straight pin will cause a little bump. Any place you have trouble keeping the fabric smooth, this tape will work wonders.

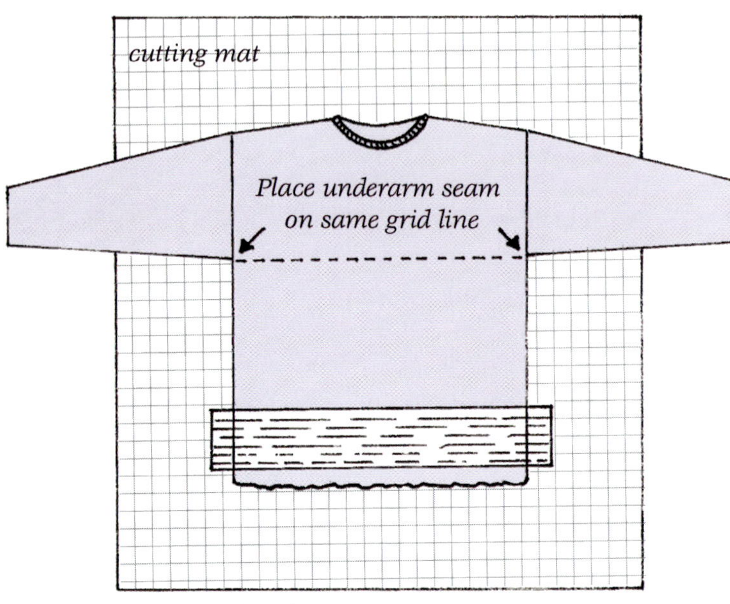

With ruler and rotary cutter cut bottom even through both thicknesses

FIG. 2. Cutting the bottom edge

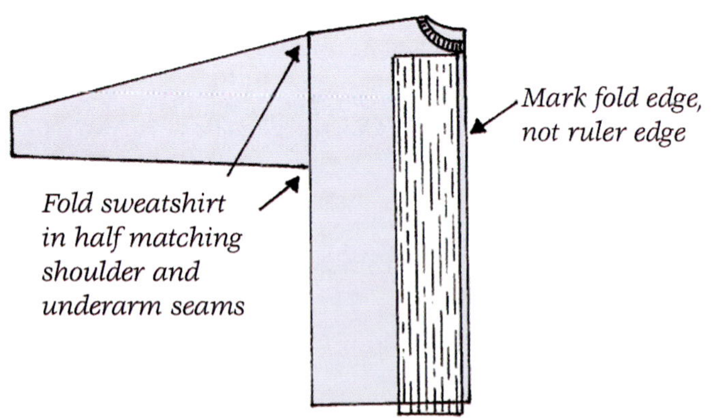

Place ruler on top of fold to stabilize sweatshirt while marking

FIG. 3. Marking the center front

Preparing the Sweatshirt

You've chosen your pattern and gathered the supplies. It's now time to start making your jacket. The following steps are common to most of the jackets in this book. However, before beginning, check your pattern for specific instructions on seam allowance and neck edges.

Remove the Bottom and Sleeve Bands

With scissors, cut off the bottom and sleeve bands following the manufacturer's stitching line. This does not have to be a straight cut at this time, but keep as much body and sleeve length as possible.

Cut the Bottom Edge Even

To cut the bottom edge straight, lay the sweatshirt flat on a large cutting mat, with the front facing up. Do not allow any of the sweatshirt to fall off the edge of the table. You want the sweatshirt completely supported. Line up both underarms on the same grid line to ensure the sweatshirt is lying straight on the mat (fig. 2). Using a long ruler and rotary cutter and leaving as much length as possible, cut the bottom edge straight. This is a critical step for a straight bottom edge. I don't recommend using scissors for this step because it's too easy to cut slightly off and the handling that is required with scissors could stretch the bottom edge.

Mark the Center Front

To find the center front, fold the sweatshirt in half, matching underarm and shoulder seams with the front facing out. Place a ruler as shown and mark along the fold (not along the ruler) with a fabric marker or chalk (fig. 3).

Cut the Center Front

To cut the center front, unfold the marked sweatshirt, and lay it flat with the front facing up, not allowing any of the sweatshirt to hang off the edge of the table. Slip a small cutting mat inside the sweatshirt. Using the marked center line as a guideline, cut the center front with a long ruler and rotary cutter (fig. 4). Please be careful! If the cutting mat does not reach from hem to neck, the back of the sweatshirt could be cut. Place a straight pin through the sweatshirt where the mat stops to remind yourself to stop cutting and shift the mat.

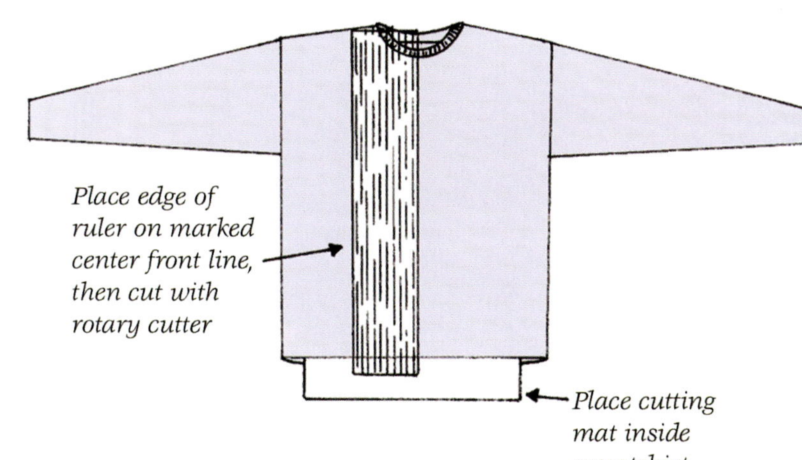

Fig. 4. Cutting the center front

Determine and Cut Hem Length

By now the sweatshirt is like a jacket. Put the sweatshirt on, and determine and mark the hem length according to the pattern instructions. Play with the length just a bit. I often recommend having a friend help with this, since it's tough to be honest with ourselves and hem length can be critical for a flattering fit. So many of us try to cover up the body parts we are self-conscious about. Strive for balance between your top and bottom half. It's best not to make the jacket so long that you lose your legs. If you have chosen the Long Tunic, cut the sweatshirt bottom at the waist, which tricks the eye and gives the illusion that everything below this line is leg.

Some sweatshirts, like the Long Tunic and the Collared Swing Jacket, will be cut much shorter than their finished length. The key here is the creation of a horizontal line. It's

Right or Left?

When the instructions refer to the right or left of the jacket, it means the right or left as you're wearing the garment (which is opposite of right and left when the sweatshirt is lying on the table as you're working on it).

best if this horizontal line does not fall at the hips, which is an unflattering placement, so cut higher than the hip line. Remember, you will be adding lots of length with the fabric, so even though it seems really short, you will be adding a lot later. Two other jackets to mention here are the Cinched Waist Jacket and the Drawstring Jacket. The hemlines will pull up some when the waist is cinched. Consider leaving about ½" extra in length on these jackets.

Once you have decided and marked where you need to trim the hem edge, use a long ruler and rotary cutter to cut off an even amount around the bottom. Don't forget to include the seam allowance.

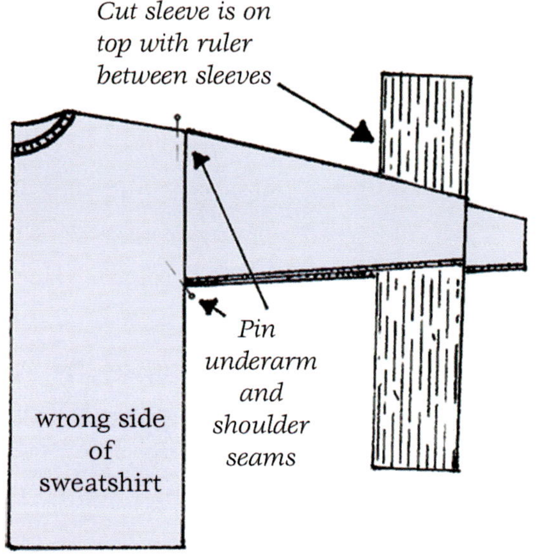

Fig. 5. Cutting the sleeve

Sleeves

Before cutting the sleeve length, check the pattern for any specific instructions and seam allowances. Some jackets may have you cut sleeve length after other steps have been completed. For instance, when making the Swing

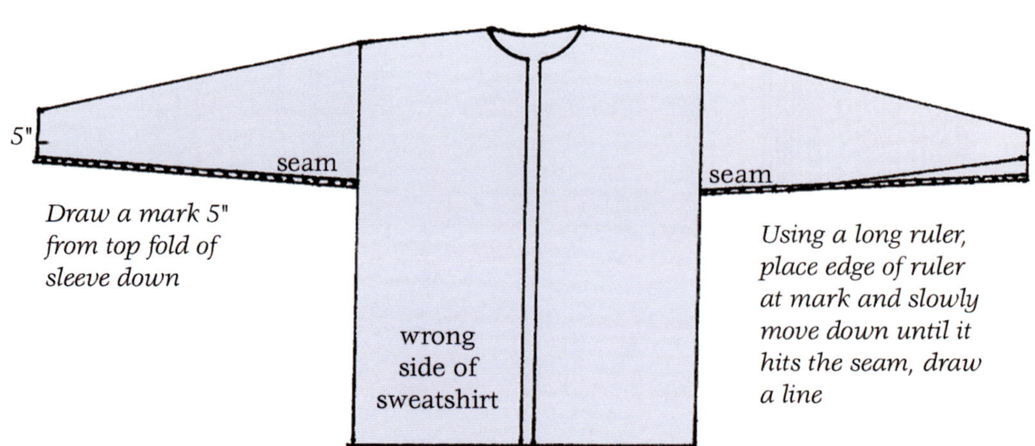

Fig. 6. Taking in the sleeve depth

Jacket with Shoulder Pleats you will need to sew in the pleats before cutting the sleeve length, since the pleats will draw up the length. Most sleeves are marked 1/4" longer than the desired finished length. But if there is additional trim, like on the Ruffled Jacket, the sleeves are cut shorter than the desired finished length. Be sure to check your pattern before marking the sleeve cutting length.

Once you have reviewed the pattern, put the jacket on, and mark the sleeve at the desired length. Traditionally the sleeve length should fall between the wrist and top thumb knuckle when your arms are to your sides. However sleeve length preference is very personal, so mark a length that is comfortable for you.

Turn the sweatshirt wrong side out and cut the sleeves one at a time. This allows you to see the underarm seam and make sure it's smooth and not twisted. Using a ruler and rotary cutter, trim off the extra length and discard the piece you have cut off. Do NOT use this trimmed piece to measure the next sleeve. To trim the second sleeve, fold the sweatshirt in half, matching shoulder and underarm seams and lay it on the table with the cut sleeve on top. Pin the underarm and shoulder seams together to ensure they stay lined up. Slip a ruler between the sleeves and, with a rotary cutter, trim the bottom sleeve to match the top sleeve (fig. 5).

Sometimes my sleeves have too much depth from the top of the sleeve to the underarm. I also find that a slimmer sleeve is more flattering on me. As always, check the pattern before proceeding. The Zip Front Jacket requires you to cut up the sides and sleeves, so wait before taking in the sleeves. If you do decide to take in your sleeves, turn the sweatshirt wrong side out and lay the sleeves out smooth. Place a mark at the wrist 5" down from the center top fold. Line up a long ruler from the mark to the underarm seam. Draw a line along the ruler's edge with a fabric marker or chalk (fig. 6). Using a basting stitch on the machine, sew on the drawn line through both thicknesses. Repeat for the other sleeve. Turn the jacket right side out and try it on. Determine if the right amount has been taken up or if additional adjustments need to be made. If you continue with taking the sleeves in, trim the excess off 1/4" below the basting stitches with a ruler and rotary cutter. Finish the sleeve seams with an overcast stitch.

Necklines

Before altering the neckline of the sweatshirt, check your pattern for any specific neck edge instructions. If the pattern instructs you to remove the neckband, use a seam ripper instead of cutting it off. This allows you to reuse the seam allowance the manufacturer used and keeps the neck opening from becoming too large. Remove the neckband with care; try not to stretch the opening excessively when removing the band. Once the neckband has been removed, press the neck edge with spray starch to stabilize it. If you choose a pattern for a collared jacket, the neckbands are not removed.

Chenille By The Inch® Strips

1. Hold Chenille By The Inch in the center and pull to remove the tear-away backing. The backing will begin to separate at the stitching lines and easily pull away. For quick removal of the backing and to keep the stitches secure, remove every other channel of the backing, pulling from the center to the edges.

Note: *The tear-away backing on Chenille By The Inch is extremely heat sensitive and should not be placed near irons or other heat-producing items.*

2. With a rotary cutter and Chenille Cutting Guide, cut the chenille into strips. Place the line of the guide directly on top of the second stitching line from one edge. Holding the guide securely, cut the chenille into ⅜" wide strips. The strips should have an equal amount of fabric on either side of the stitched line.

3. Using your preferred fabric marking method and referring to the project patterns, transfer the chenille placement lines to the background fabric.

Sew the chenille strips to the background by aligning the center stitching line of the strip with the transferred pattern line. Do not cut the length of the strips until they are sewn in place. Chenille By The Inch can be sewn directly to the background fabric without pinning or basting. Because chenille is sewn on the bias, avoid stretching the strips as you sew them in place.

You can use every inch of Chenille By The Inch. Create continuous lines of chenille as you complete each strip by overlapping the strip ¼" with the end of a new strip, backstitch, and continue sewing. Always backstitch to secure a new strip thoroughly. Pause with your needle in the down position to keep from pulling the strip off center.

3

4. Brushing is an essential part of creating full, fluffy chenille. Once the project is completely sewn with no raw edges exposed, give a section of the sewn strips a quick overall brushing to roughen the edges. Next, lightly spray that section with distilled water and 2–3 drops of fabric softener. Brush again. Once the piece is brushed and dried, the chenille will be full and fluffy. For maximum bloom, launder the finished project to wash out all the sizing.

Note: *When working with background fabrics that may be sensitive to brushing, such as flannels, knits, and textured fabrics, transfer the appliqué pattern and chenille placement lines to a tear-away stabilizer. Matching the appliquéd pattern, pin the stabilizer to the background fabric. Sew the chenille on top of the stabilizer and background fabric. Brush the chenille before removing the stabilizer.*

4

Patterns

18
30
23

Collared Swing Jacket

Collared Swing Jacket

Materials

Beige sweatshirt

Five ⅞" buttons

Basic supplies as listed on page 9

Fabric Requirements and Cutting Instructions

- ⅓ yard each of 6 assorted blue prints
  - 3 strips 2" x WOF from each for bottom, collar, and cuffs (total 18)
  - 2 strips 3½" x WOF from one for the center front placket
- ½–⅞ yard* coordinating lining fabric
  - 1–2* strips 10½" x WOF for bottom lining
  - 1 strip 4½" x 30" for collar lining
  - 2 strips 2½" x 20" for cuff lining
- 1¼–1⅞* yards woven, fusible interfacing
  - 2–4* strips 10" x WOF for bottom
  - 4 strips 3" x WOF for center front placket
  - 2 strips 4" x 30" for collar
  - 2 strips 2" x 19½" for cuffs

*You'll need more if the sweatshirt bottom edge measurement is greater than 40".

Making the Jacket

Step 1 Preparing the Sweatshirt

With scissors, cut off the bottom and sleeve bands from the sweatshirt. Do not remove the neck band. Mark the center front of the sweatshirt and cut from hem to neck edge. Try the sweatshirt on and mark the hem length 9¾" *shorter* than the desired finished length and the sleeve length ¼" *longer* than the desired length. Trim the hem and sleeves. (See Preparing the Sweatshirt pages 10–13.)

Sew 2" x WOF strips together (make 3)

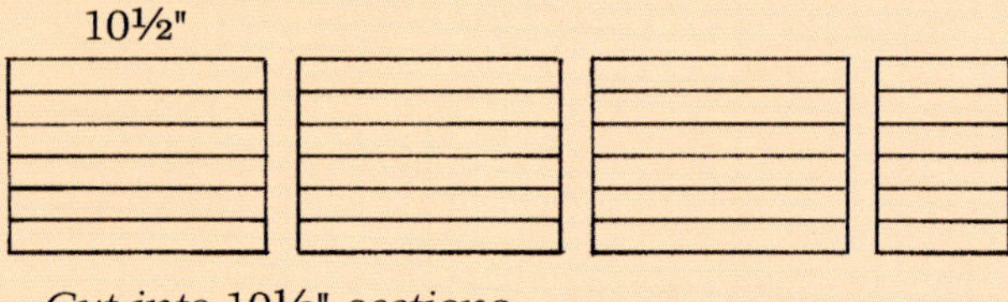

Cut into 10½" sections

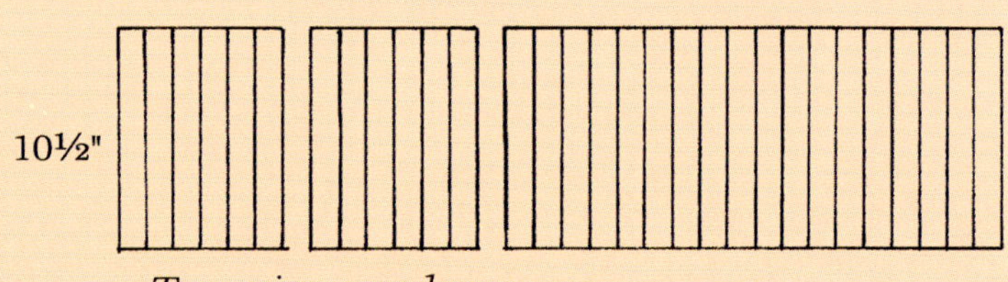

Turn pieces and sew

Fig. 1. Extention piecing

Step 2 Making the Extensions

Make 3 strip-sets with the assorted 2" x WOF strips (fig. 1). Press. Measure the bottom raw edge of the sweatshirt. Cut the strip-sets into enough 10½" sections to exceed this measurement. Sew the sections together as shown. Add ½" to the sweatshirt bottom edge measurement and cut a piece that size. Center the cut so that the two strips that will fall at the center front (the two at the ends) are equal in size.

Step 3 Adding the Extensions

Cut the coordinating 10½" x WOF lining to the same size as the bottom pieced section, joining two strips if needed. Center and fuse one (or two) 10" x WOF interfacing strips to the wrong side of both the bottom pieced section and the lining. With *right* sides together, sew one long edge of the pieced section and lining together. Turn right sides out and press. Tape under the remaining long edge of the pieced section (see page 9).

Pin the *right* side of the lining to the *wrong* side of the sweatshirt bottom raw edge, matching the center front edges, and sew with a ¼" seam. Press the seam toward the bottom section. Match the taped edge of the pieced section with the stitching line and topstitch in place.

Step 4 Center Front

Center a 3" x WOF piece of interfacing on the wrong side of a 3½" x WOF placket strip and fuse in place. Sew the *right* side of the fabric strip to the *wrong* side of a center front edge, leaving at least ½" extending beyond the hem edge. Trim the end to ½" and trim the other end so it extends only ¼" beyond the neck band.

Tape under the remaining long edge of the center front strip. Press the strip to the right side, matching the taped edge with the stitching line and tucking in both ends (fig. 2). (The center front placket should be ¼" shorter than the neck band edge.) Topstitch the placket in place along the taped edge. Hand stitch the small openings at the hem and neck closed. Repeat for the opposite center front placket.

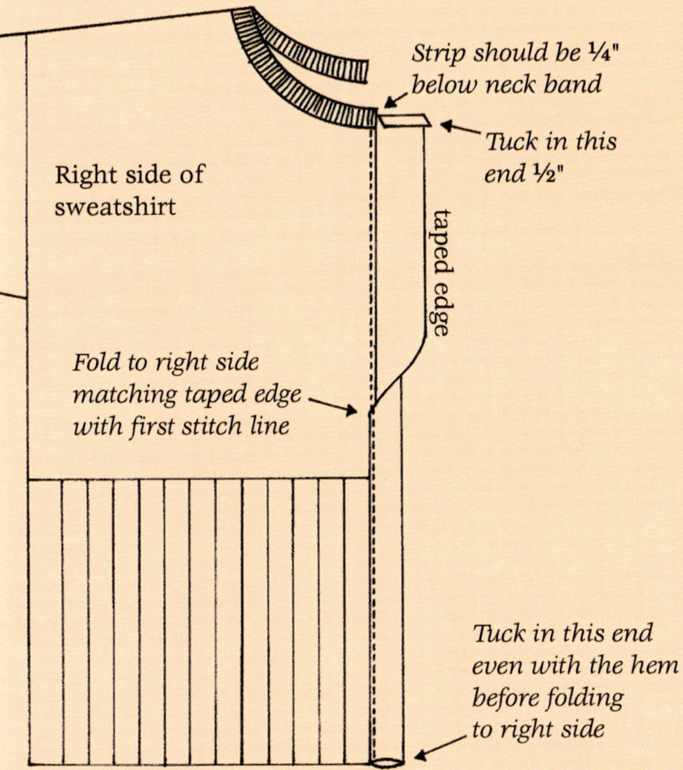

Fig. 2. Center front placket

Step 5 Measuring the Collar

Cut 2 pieces 4½" x 15" for the collar from the remaining extension strip-sets. Pin the collar pieces to the neckband, starting at the center front and extending ¼" beyond each center front placket seam (fig. 3). Be careful not to stretch the neckband. Allow the excess collar fabric to fall to the center back. At the center back mark where the collar sections meet using a pin or fabric marker. Remove the collar pieces from the neckband. Measure ¼" beyond the marks and trim the excess fabric at the center back. Sew the two sections together and press.

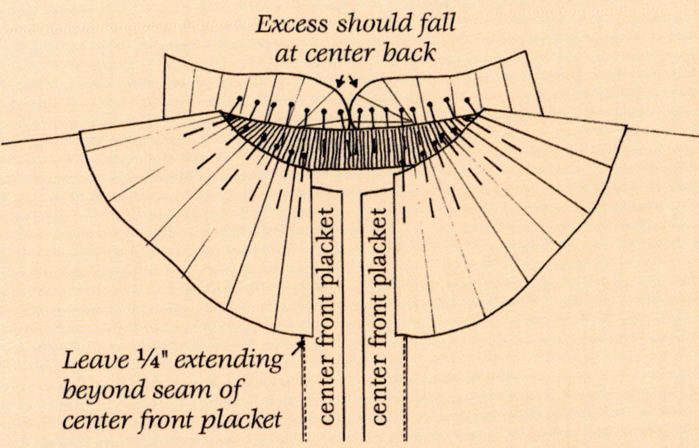

Fig. 3. Pinning collar to neckband

Step 6 Making the Collar

Trim the coordinating 4½" x 30" collar lining to match the pieced collar. Trim the woven fusible interfacing 4" x 30" pieces ½" smaller than the collar and lining. Center and fuse to the wrong side of both the collar and lining. Tape under one long edge of the collar. With *right* sides together sew the collar and collar lining together on three sides, leaving the side with the taped edge open. Trim the corners, turn right side out, and press.

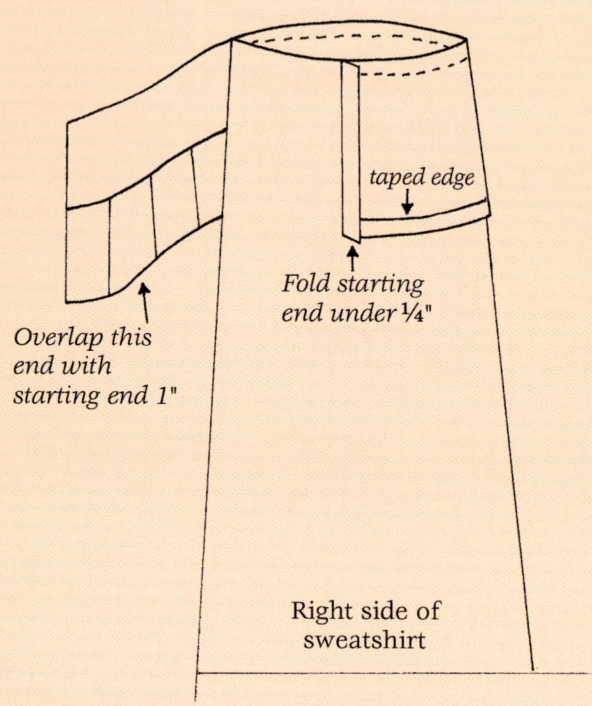

Fig. 4. Cuff

Step 7 Applying the Collar

Sew the collar lining to the right side of the neckband, matching the side collar seams to the center front placket seams. Press the seam allowance toward the lining. Pin the taped edge of the collar to the neckband, matching the first stitching line. Topstitch in place along the taped edge. Try on the jacket to determine the proper collar fold. Fold the collar over and press.

Step 8 Cuffs

Cut 2 cuff pieces 2½" x 20" from the remaining extension strip-sets. Center and fuse the 2" x 19½" interfacing pieces to the wrong side of both the pieced cuffs and the cuff linings. With *right* sides together, sew each cuff and cuff lining together along one long edge. Tape under the remaining long edge of the pieced cuffs.

Press one end of the cuff and lining under ¼" (fig. 4). Sew the cuff lining to the sleeve edge, *right* sides together, starting with the pressed end and overlapping the finishing end 1". Trim off the excess and press the seam allowance toward the cuff. Match the taped edge with the stitching line and topstitch the cuff in place. Hand stitch the overlap closed. Repeat for the opposite cuff. Fold up the cuff.

Step 9 Buttonholes

Mark buttonhole placement for 5 buttons on the right (as you're wearing the jacket) center front placket. Make the buttonholes and sew the buttons on the opposite placket.

Swing Jacket with Shoulder Pleats

Swing Jacket with Shoulder Pleats

Materials

Beige sweatshirt

Two 1" buttons

Basic supplies as listed on page 9

Fabric Requirements and Cutting Instructions

- 1/3 yard beige/rust/green stripe
  - Four side godets (pattern is on page 29)
  - Four sleeve godets
  - One button loop 1½" x 6" bias
- 1/3 yard rust polka dot
  - One 1½" x 30" bias for neck edge (can be pieced)
  - Two 1½" x WOF for hem
  - Two 1½" x WOF for center fronts
  - One 1½" x WOF for sleeve trim
- 1/3 yard woven, fusible interfacing
  - Four side godet patterns
  - Four sleeve godet patterns

Making the Jacket

Step 1 Preparing the Sweatshirt

With scissors, cut off the bottom and sleeve bands from the sweatshirt. Remove the neckband with a seam ripper. Lay the sweatshirt flat and mark the sides from hem to underarm. Mark the center front of the sweatshirt and cut from hem to neck edge. Try on the jacket, mark the hem length ¼" *longer* than the desired length, and trim the hem. (See Preparing the Sweatshirt pages 10–13.)

Step 2 Shoulder Pleats

Mark shoulder pleats on the front and back parallel to the center front and center back (fig. 1).

Tape the marked pleat lines (fig. 2) using water-soluble basting tape (page 9). Remove the paper from the tape, bring the outside lines of the pleat to the center line, and stick in place; press.

Topstitch the pleat in place as shown (fig. 3, page 26).

Step 3 Sleeve Length

Try on the jacket and mark the sleeve length ¼" *longer* than the desired finished length. Trim the sleeve length as marked. Cut the sweatshirt at the side marks from hem to underarm. Turn the sweatshirt wrong side out, and trim off the sleeve seam from the underarm to the wrist edge, opening the sweatshirt completely.

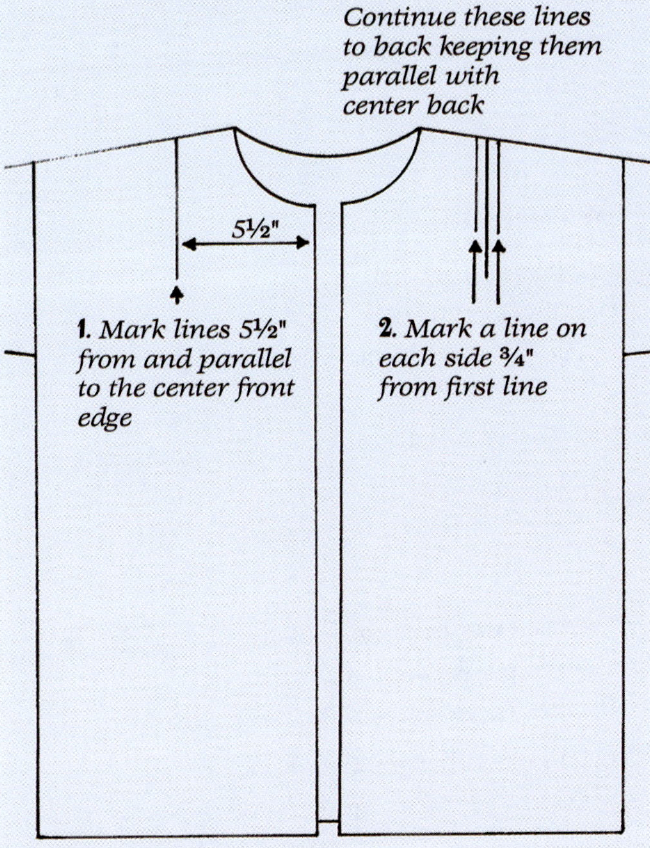

FIG. 1. Mark shoulder pleats.

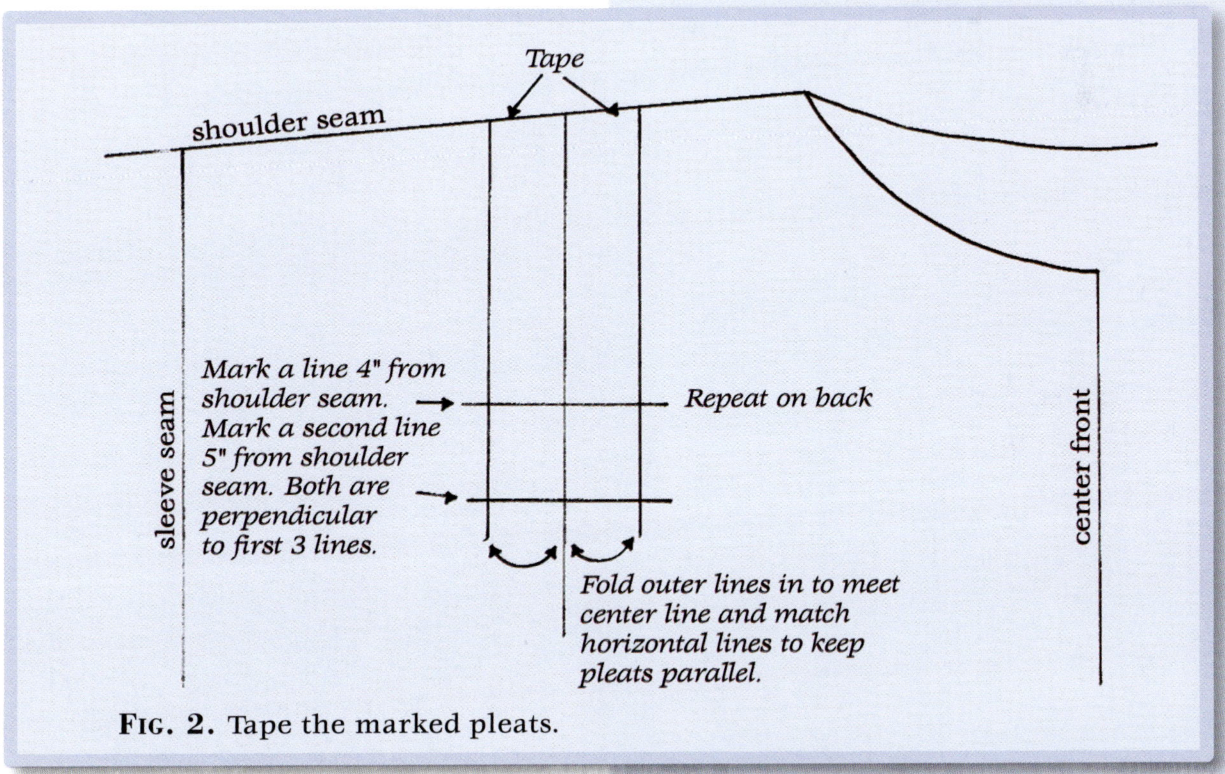

FIG. 2. Tape the marked pleats.

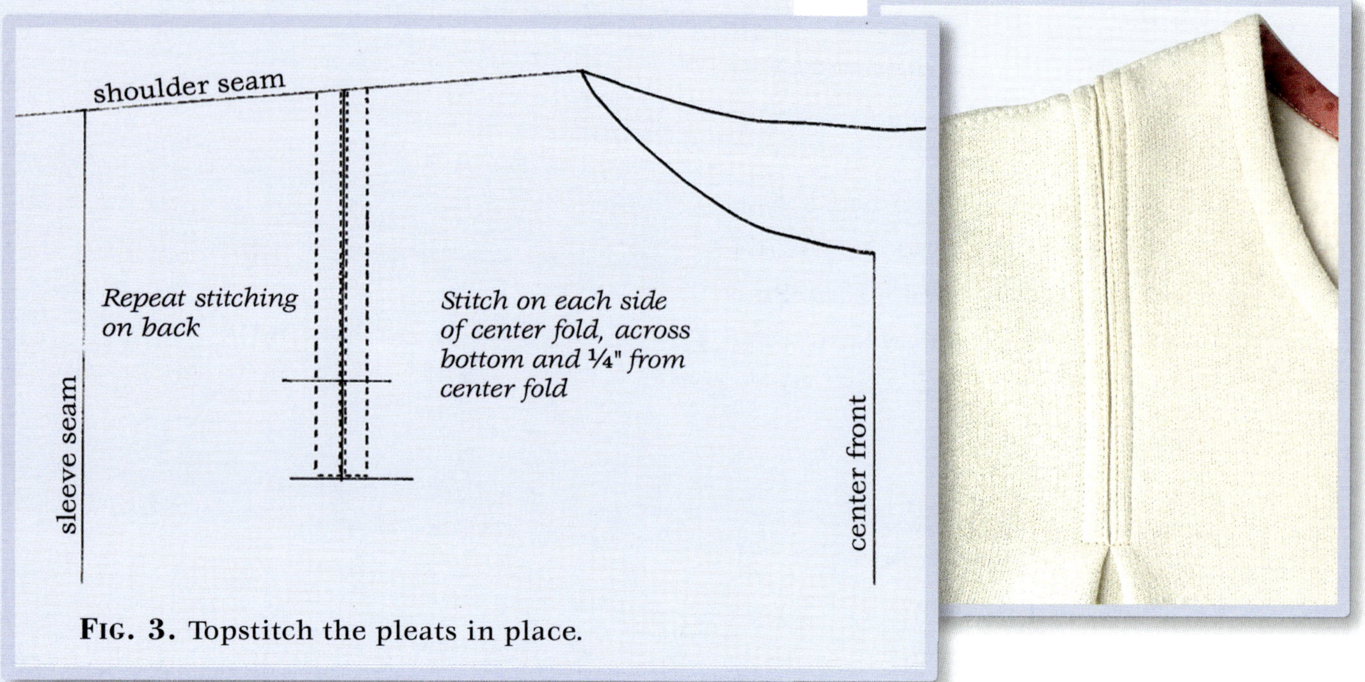

Fig. 3. Topstitch the pleats in place.

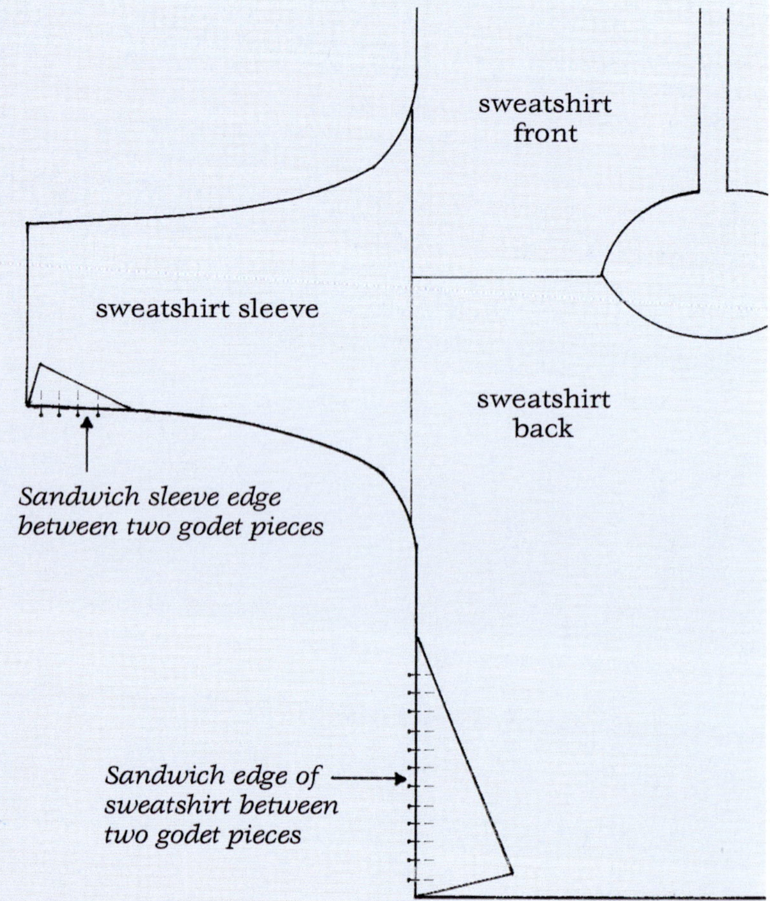

Fig. 4. Pin godets in place.

Step 4 Godet Insertion

Fuse one piece of interfacing to the wrong side of each godet piece. Sandwich the back side raw edge of the sweatshirt between two side godet pieces at the hem, with the right sides of the godets toward the sweatshirt; pin in place (fig. 4). Repeat at the other back side and at both wrists with the sleeve godets.

Sew the godets in place stopping at the marked dots. Press the godets away from the sweatshirt, *wrong* sides together.

Pin the sweatshirt, *right* sides together, matching the underarm seams, hem, and wrist edges, pinning through both godets (fig. 5). Sew from the wrist to the hem on both sides. Press the seam toward the godet. Overcast stitch the seam.

Step 5 Hem

Sew two 1½" x WOF polka dot strips together, end-to-end, and press the seam open. Press the strip in half, *wrong* sides together, and matching the long raw edges. With *right* sides together and matching both raw edges of the folded strip to the edge of the sweatshirt hem, sew in place. Press the strip to the wrong side of the sweatshirt and topstitch in place along the folded edge. Trim the ends even with the center front.

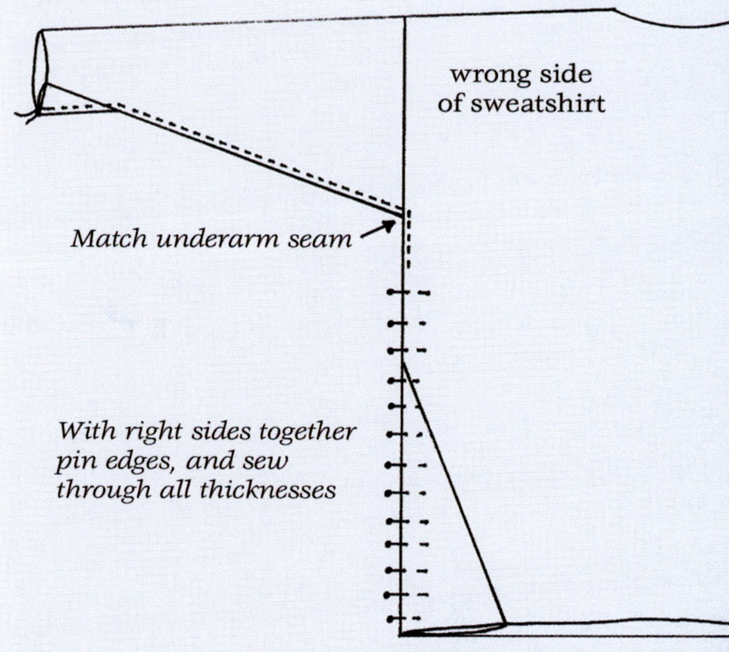

Fig. 5. Pin through sweatshirt and godets.

Step 6 Center Front

Tape under one long edge of a 1½" x WOF polka dot strip. Sew the strip to the center front, *right* sides together, leaving at least ½" extending beyond the neck and hem. Trim the ends to ½". Press the strip to the wrong side, tucking in the ends at the hem, and stitch in place along the taped edge. Trim even with the neck edge. Hand stitch the small opening at the hem closed. Repeat for the opposite center front.

Step 7 Neck Edge

Press a 1½" x 30" polka dot bias strip in half, *wrong* sides together and matching the long raw edges. Sew to the neck edge, *right* sides together and leaving at least ½" extending beyond the center fronts. Trim the ends to ½" at the center front, tuck in the ends, and press to the wrong side. Stitch in place along the folded edge. Hand stitch the small openings at the center front closed.

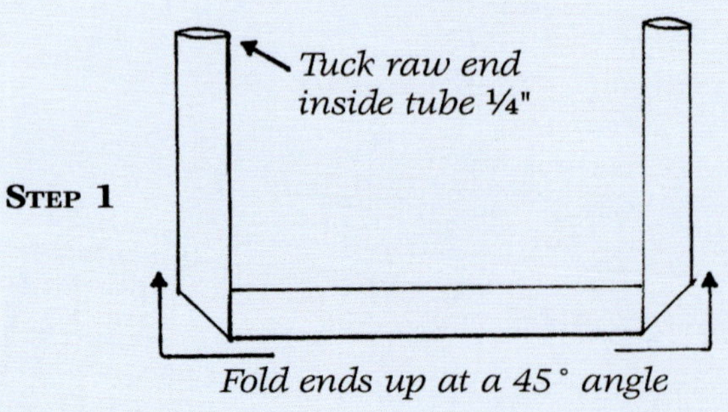

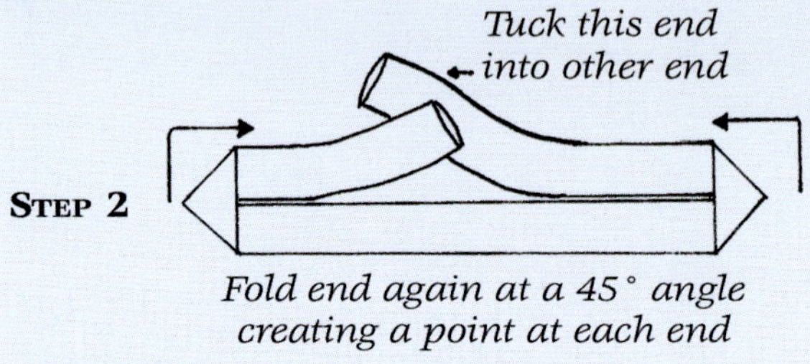

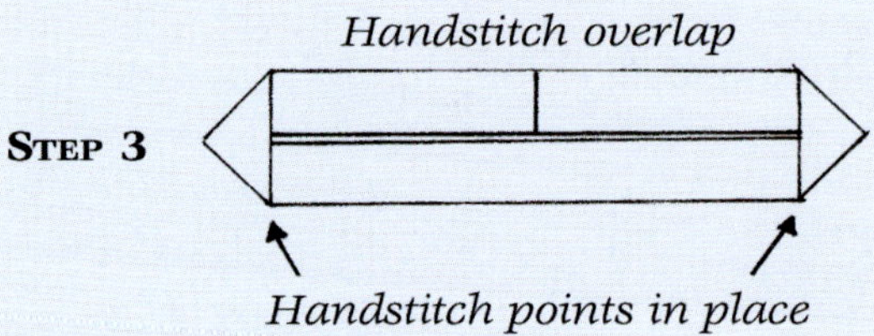

Fig. 6. Button loop

Step 8 Sleeve Trim

Press a 1½" x WOF polka dot strip in half, wrong sides together and matching the long raw edges. Press one end of the strip under ¼". With *right* sides together and matching the raw edges, sew the strip to the sleeve, starting at the pressed end and overlapping ½" at the finish. Trim off the excess and press the strip to the *wrong* side. Topstitch the strip along the folded edge. Hand stitch the small opening at the overlap closed. Repeat for the opposite sleeve.

Step 9 Button Loop

Sew a 1½" x 6" bias strip, *right* sides together and matching the long raw edges, forming a tube. Turn right side out. Press the seam to the center back. Fold and press the button loop and hand stitch the folds in place (fig. 6). Sew one end of the button loop to the right front of the jacket (as you're wearing the jacket) at the neck edge. Sew a button at one end. Sew the second button to the opposite center front.

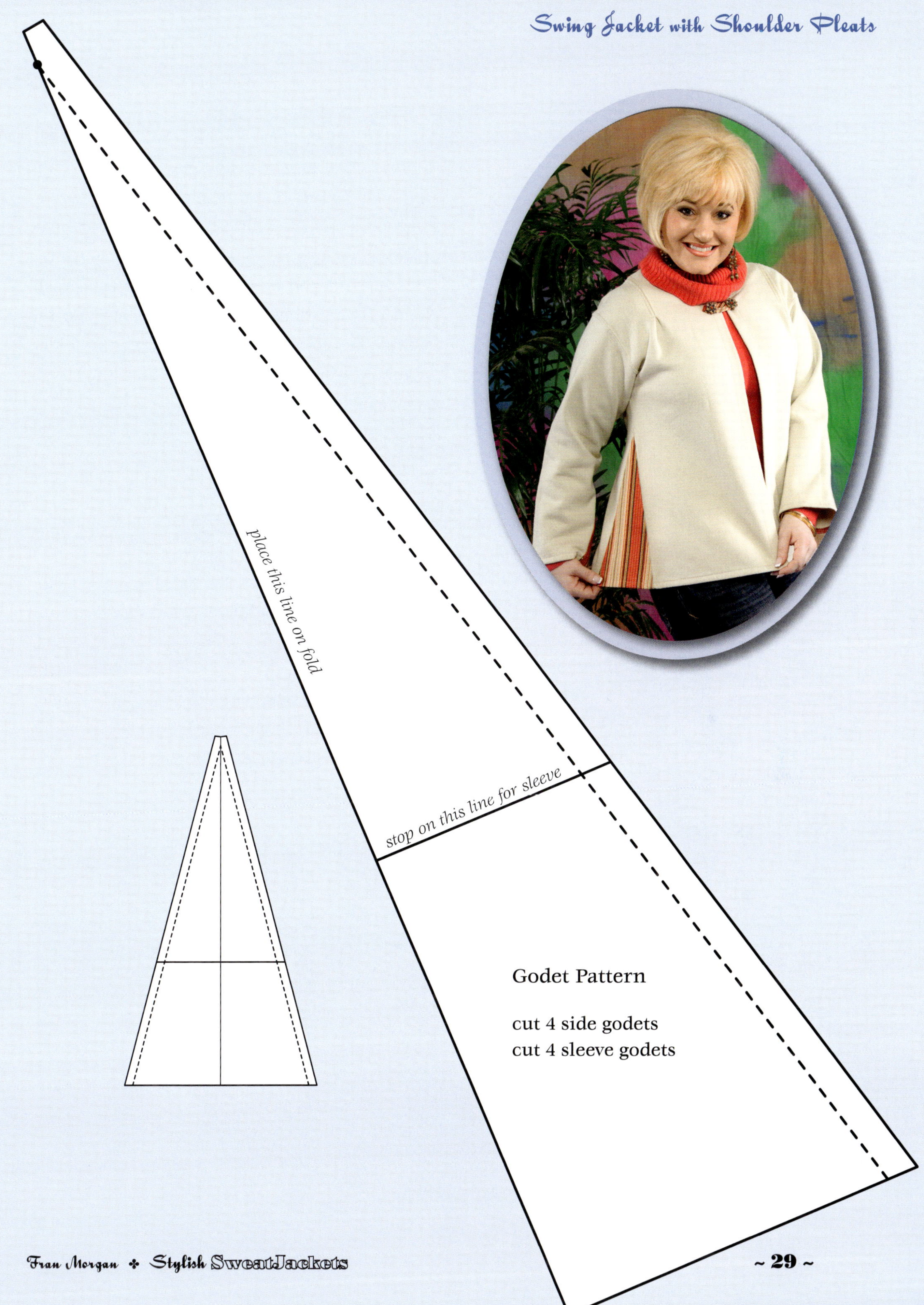
place this line on fold
stop on this line for sleeve
Godet Pattern
cut 4 side godets
cut 4 sleeve godets

Zip Front Jacket

Zip Front Jacket

Materials

Brown sweatshirt
200" of eggplant Chenille By The Inch
200" of wine Chenille By The Inch
200" of chocolate Chenille By The Inch
Chenille Brush
Chenille Cutting Guide
Spray bottle with water
22" multicolored separating zipper
1 yard lightweight, paper-backed fusible web
Masking tape
Basic supplies as listed on page 9

Fabric Requirements and Cutting Instructions

- ⅔ yard red gradation fabric
  - One 1½" x 30" bias for neck (can be pieced)
  - One 1¼" x 20" bias for side slits
  - Two 5½" x WOF for center front facing
  - Two 1½" x WOF for hem
  - One 1½" x WOF for sleeves
- ½ yard topaz (brown) organza
  - Approximately six 2½" x WOF for stripes
- ½ yard copper organza
  - Approximately six 2½" x WOF for stripes
- ½ yard burnt orange organza
  - Approximately six 2½" x WOF for stripes
- ⅛ yard woven, fusible interfacing
  - Three 1" x WOF strips

Ironing Note

Use the silk setting on the iron for this entire sweatshirt. If the iron is too hot, it will melt the organza!

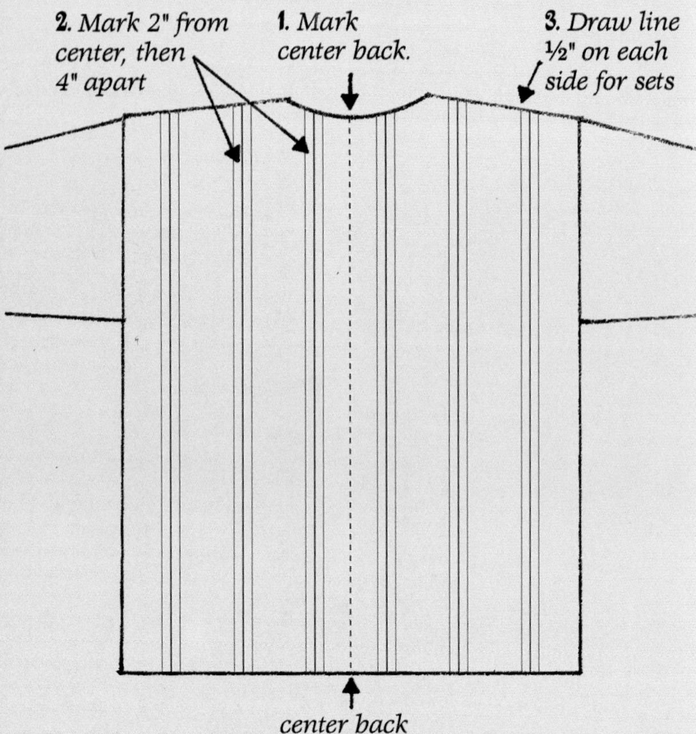

FIG. 1. Organza placement

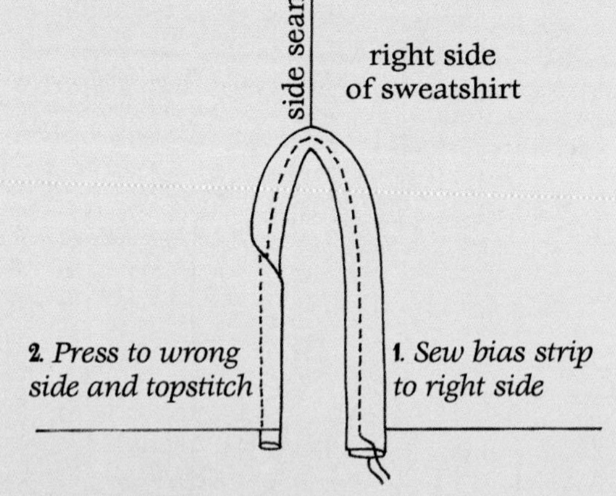

FIG. 2. Side slit

Making the Jacket

Step 1 Preparing the Sweatshirt

With scissors, cut off the bottom and sleeve bands from the sweatshirt. Remove the neckband with a seam ripper. Mark the center front of the sweatshirt and cut from the hem to the neck edge. Try on the sweatshirt and mark the hem and sleeve lengths ¼" *longer* than the desired finished length. Trim the hem and sleeves. (See Preparing the Sweatshirt pages 10–13.)

Lay the sweatshirt flat, matching the center fronts, and mark the sides from hem to underarm. Cut the sides on the marked lines. Turn the sweatshirt *wrong* side out, and cut off the sleeve seams from underarm to sleeve edge, opening the sweatshirt completely.

Step 2 Organza Placement

Find the center back by folding the sweatshirt in half, matching the shoulder and underarms. Mark the center back from neck edge to hem. Draw a line 2" on both sides of the center back line. Continue drawing vertical lines 4" apart (fig. 1). (Erase or cross through the center back line; it is for positioning only.) Turn the sweatshirt over and draw a line 2" from each center front, then more lines 4" apart.

In the same way, fold the sleeves in half, matching the cut seam lines, and mark the sleeve center. Draw more lines 4" apart.

At each drawn line on the body and sleeves, add a line ½" on both sides to create sets of 3 lines.

Step 3 Organza Strips

To determine the number of organza strips of each color, count your line sets and divide by three. (I had a total of 18 sets, so I needed 6 strips of each of 3 colors.) Cut the organza strips 2½" x WOF. Fold the strips in half, *wrong* sides together and matching the long raw edges, and sew, forming a tube. Press the seam to the center back. Cut one ¾" x WOF strip of lightweight, paper-backed fusible web for each tube. Adhere the fusible web to the seam side of the tubes. Remove the paper and adhere to the jacket, centering the organza on the marked line sets, alternating the colors, and tucking in the ends ½" at the shoulder and sleeve seams. Topstitch the organza in place along both edges.

Step 4 Adding Chenille to the Sleeves

Prepare Chenille By The Inch for application (see pages 14–15). On the sleeves, sew chocolate chenille to the center of the copper organza strips, eggplant chenille to the burnt orange organza, and wine chenille to the topaz organza, back-tacking at the beginning and end of each strip to secure and overlapping the ends to add a new strip as needed. With *right* sides together and matching the underarm seams, pin the side and sleeve seam from the wrist to 4" above the hem. Sew with an overcast stitch leaving 4" at the bottom open for a side slit. Repeat for the opposite side.

Step 5 Side Slit

For the side slit, press a 1¼" x 20" bias strip in half, *wrong* sides together and matching the long raw edges. Sew the folded strip to the right side of the slit, press to the wrong side, and topstitch in place (fig. 2). Trim off the excess length even with the bottom raw edge. Repeat for the opposite side slit.

Step 6 Hem

Center a 1" x WOF interfacing on the *wrong* side of the two 1½" x WOF hem strips and fuse in place. Cut one strip in half for the front hems. With *right* sides together, sew the strips to the bottom edges of the sweatshirt, leaving ½" extending beyond the side slit edges. Trim the center front edges even with the sweatshirt. Tape under the unsewn long edge of the hem (page 9). Trim the ends at the side slits to ½", tuck in the ends, and press the strips to the wrong side. Stitch in place along the taped edge. Hand stitch the small openings at the side slits closed.

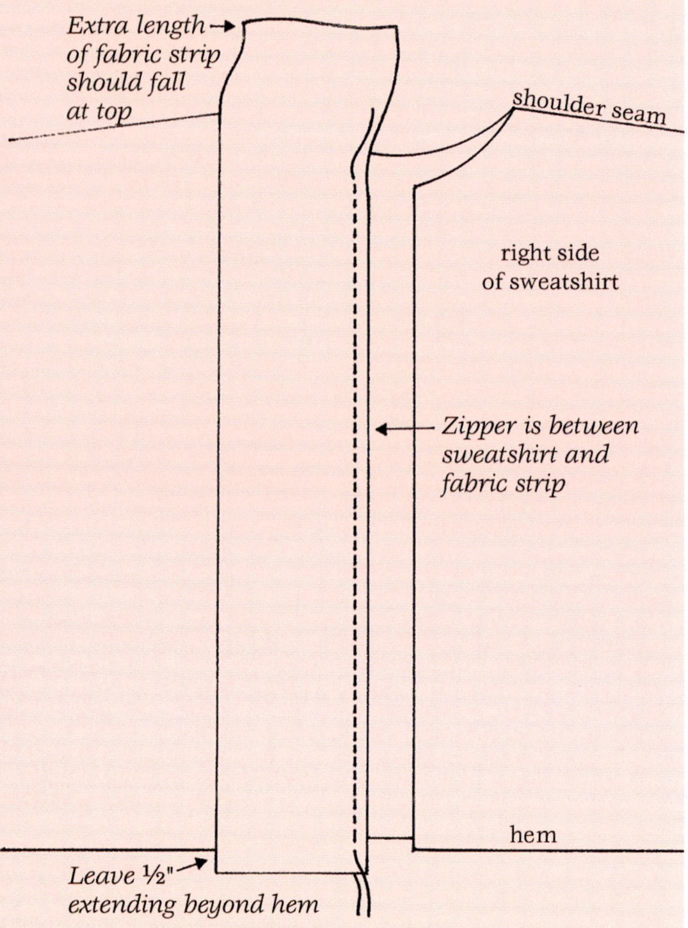

Fig. 3. Zipper center front

Step 7 Zipper

Separate the zipper. With *right* sides together, position the left side of the zipper face down on the right center front (as you're wearing the jacket) ¼" from the bottom edge, matching the center front edges and allowing any excess to fall at the neck. Baste in place. With *right* sides together, position a 5½" x WOF facing along the center front edge, matching the raw edges and sandwiching the zipper, leaving ½" extending beyond the bottom edge. Sew in place (fig. 3).

Tape under the remaining long edge of the facing. Press the facing to the wrong side, tucking in the bottom ½". Trim the facing ½" longer than the shoulder seam, press under ½" at the shoulder, and stitch the facing in place along the taped edge and shoulder fold. Trim the facing to match the neck edge. If needed, trim the zipper ½" longer than the neck edge. Topstitch the front edge of the sweatshirt next to the zipper. Hand stitch the opening at the hem closed. Repeat for the opposite center front (fig. 4).

Step 8 Neck Edge

Press the 1½" x 30" bias strip in half, *wrong* sides together and matching the long raw edges. Sew to the neck edge, *right* sides together, leaving at least ½" extending beyond each center front. Trim the excess to ½", tuck in the ends, tuck in the ends of the zipper, and turn the strip to the wrong side. Stitch the strip in place along the folded edge. Hand stitch the small openings at the center front closed.

Step 9 Sleeve Edge

Tape under one long edge of the 1½" x WOF sleeve strip. Press one end under ¼". With *right* sides together, matching raw edges and starting with the pressed-under end, sew to the sleeve edge, overlapping the finishing end 1". Trim off the excess. Press the strip to the wrong side. Stitch in place along the taped edge. Hand stitch the small opening at the overlap closed. Repeat for the opposite sleeve using the remaining length of the strip, pressing under one end ¼" before stitching as before.

Step 10 Adding Chenille to the Jacket

On the body of the jacket, sew chocolate chenille to the center of the copper organza strips, eggplant chenille to the burnt orange organza, and wine chenille to the topaz organza, back-tacking at the beginning and end of each strip to secure and overlapping the ends to add a new strip.

Step 11 Fluffing the Chenille

Using masking tape, tape on either side of the chenille strips to protect the organza. Using a spray bottle with water, dampen the sewn Chenille By The Inch strips and brush vigorously with a Chenille Brush to fluff chenille. Remove the tape.

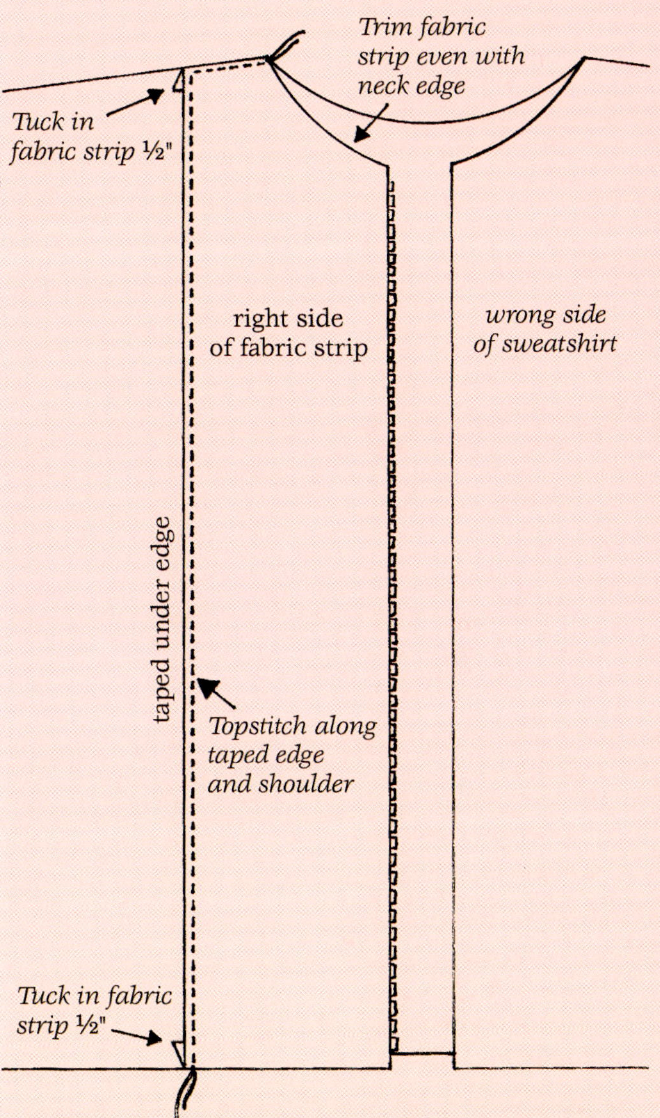

Fig. 4. Topstitch center front

Cinched Waist Jacket

Chinched Waist Jacket

Materials

Black sweatshirt

50" of Spice Chenille By The Inch

Chenille Brush

Chenille Cutting Guide

Spray bottle with water

Small amount paper-backed fusible web

One 1" button for the front

Two 9⁄16" black buttons for the sleeves

Long string to determine waist

Small amount of pattern tracing material (or tissue paper)

Ruler with 1⁄8" lines

Basic supplies as listed on page 9

Fabric Requirements and Cutting Instructions

- 2⁄3 yard black
  - One 1½" x 40" bias for neck (can be pieced)
  - Two 1½" x 12" bias for sleeve slit
  - Two 1½" x WOF for center fronts
  - Two 1½" x WOF for hem
  - Two curved front facings from pattern
  - One 1½" x WOF for sleeves
  - Three 1¼" x 6" for button loops
  - Two 3½" x WOF for waistband
- 1⁄8 yard dark red
  - Eight flower patterns from pattern
- 1⁄8 yard woven, fusible interfacing
  - Three 1" x WOF strips

Making the Jacket

Step 1 Preparing the Sweatshirt

With scissors, cut off the bottom and sleeve bands from the sweatshirt. Remove the neckband with a seam ripper. Mark the center front of the sweatshirt and cut from the hem to the neck edge. Try on the sweatshirt and mark the hem and sleeve lengths ¼" *longer* than the desired finished length. Trim the hem and sleeves. (See Preparing the Sweatshirt pages 10–13.)

Mark and cut a V-neck (fig. 1, page 38).

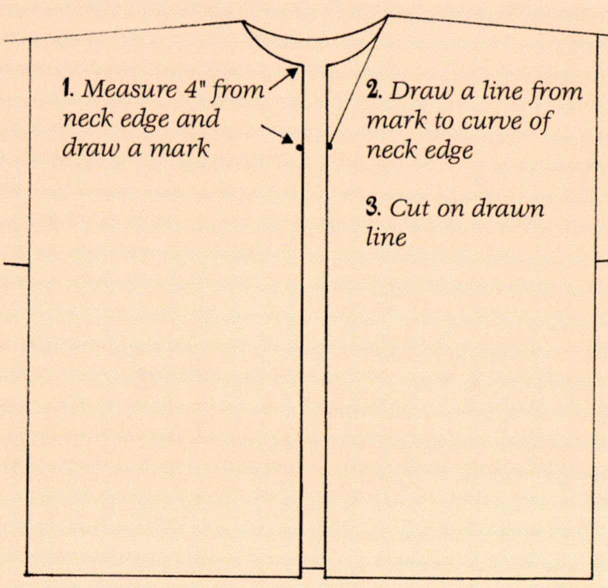

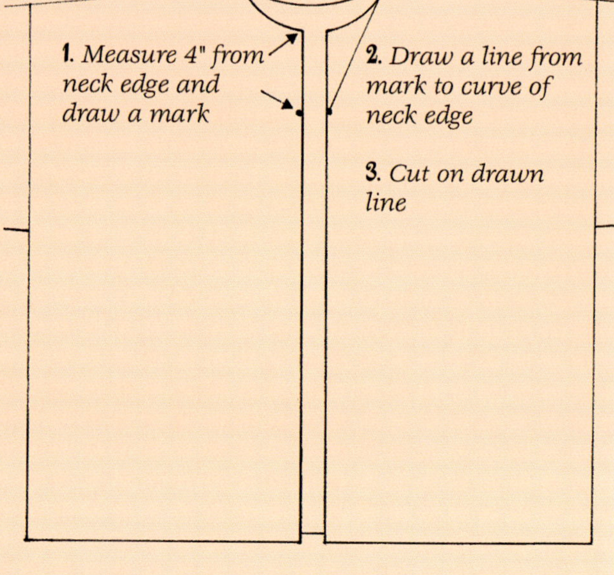

FIG. 1. Marking the v-neck

Step 2 Waistband Placement

To determine the waistband placement, try on the sweatshirt and tie a string around your waist. Place a dot at each side at the string. This dot should be at your waist. (Mine fell 4" below the underarm seam.) Remove the sweatshirt, lay it flat, and draw a line around the sweatshirt at these dots, then draw another line 1½" below the first line. This is the waistband placement (fig. 2).

Step 3 Pleats

Find the center back of the sweatshirt by folding it in half, matching the shoulder and underarm seams. Mark the center back at the waist. Draw a vertical mark at the waistband 5½" on both sides of the center back. Draw a line 1" on both sides of these marks. Fold at the outer lines and bring in to match the center marks at the waist (fig. 3). Press and hold the

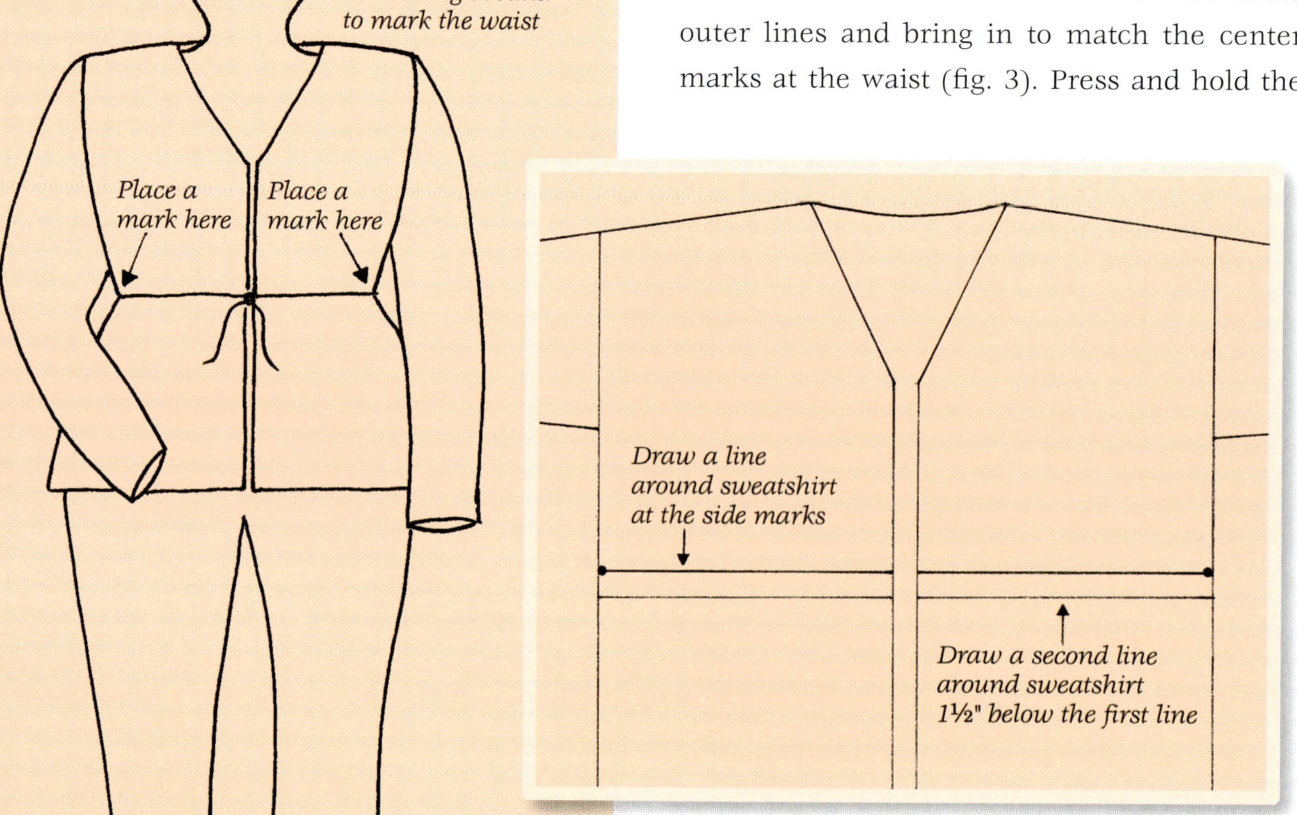

FIG. 2. Marking the waistband placement

pleats in place with wash-away tape (page 9). Sew across the top and bottom of the pleats just inside the two marked waistband lines. Repeat this process for front pleats, measuring 5½" from the center front raw edge.

Step 4 Waistband

For the waistband, sew two 3½" x WOF pieces together end-to-end. Fold in half, *right* sides together and matching the long raw edges. Sew to form a tube. Turn right side out and press with the seam at the center back of the tube. With the seam toward the sweatshirt, position the tube along the waistband placement lines. Tape in place, covering the pleat stitching. Topstitch in place along both edges. Trim the excess even with the center fronts.

Step 5 Button Loops

Make three button loops (fig. 4). Sew a 1½" x 6" bias strip, *right* sides together and matching the long raw edges, forming a tube. Turn right side out. Press the seam to the center back. Press the points only in the two sleeve loops and hand stitch the point in place. Set aside.

Pin the waistband button loop to the right front (as you're wearing the jacket) waistband, matching the raw ends of the button loop with the raw edge of the center front, with the loop pointing away from the center front. Position the ends ½" apart, leaving enough space in the loop for a 1" button. Baste in place. Trim the excess.

Step 6 Cutting the Curved Front

Trace the curve pattern onto pattern tracing material (page 44). Cut out the pattern on the traced lines. Pin the paper patterns to the

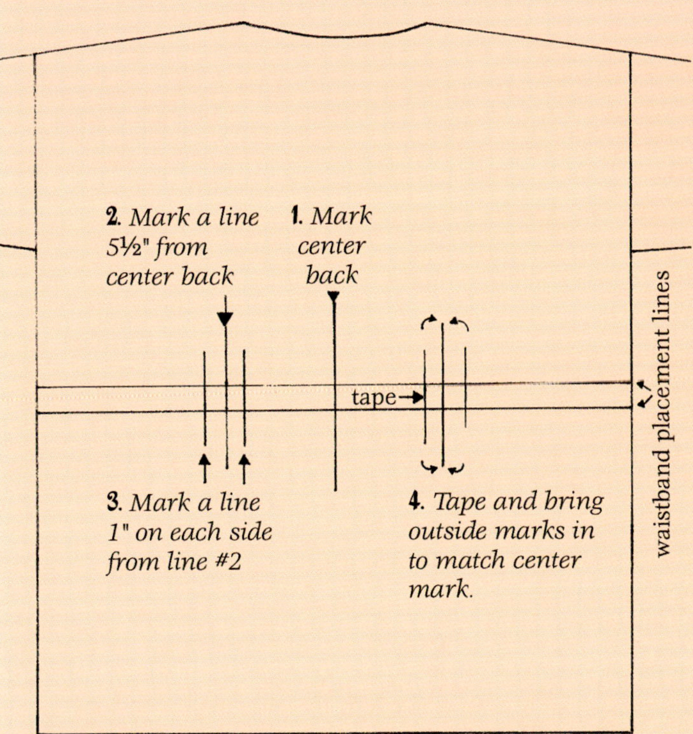

Fig. 3. Marking the pleats

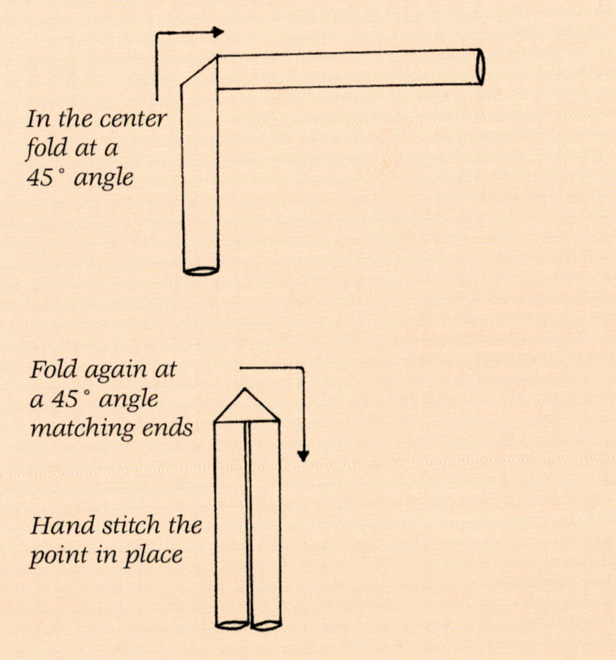

Fig. 4. Making button loops

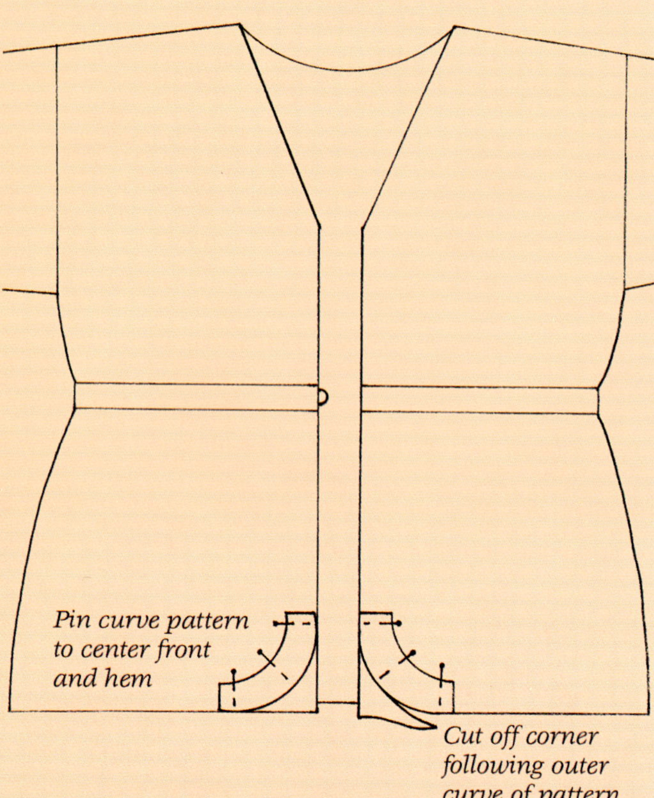

Fig. 5. Cutting the curved front

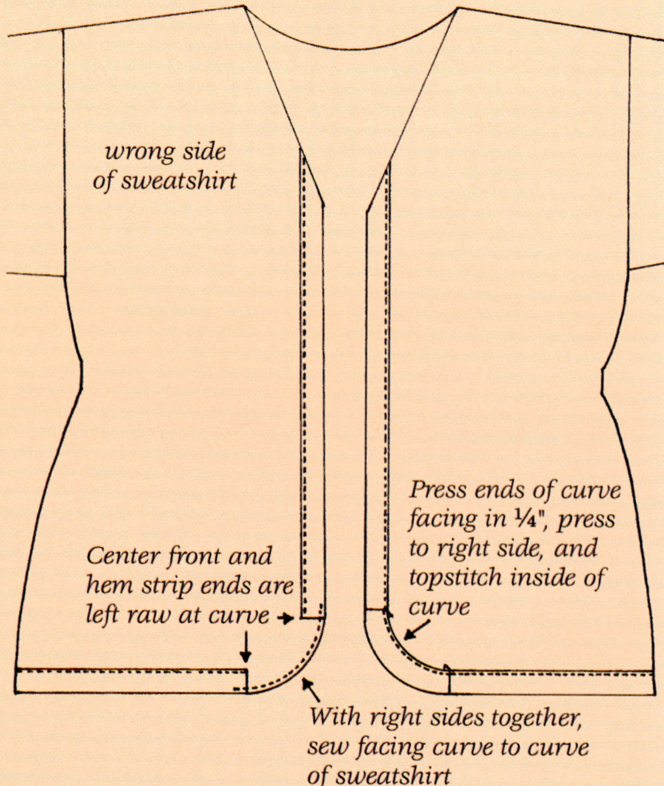

Fig. 6. Curve facing

center fronts at the bottom edge, lining up the vertical and horizontal ends with the center front and hem (fig. 5). Cut the sweatshirt along the pattern curve.

Step 7 Hem

Fuse 1" x WOF interfacing to the wrong side of the hem, ¼" above the bottom raw edge, overlapping ends of interfacing to add another strip as necessary and stopping at the curve. Sew 1½" x WOF black hem facing strips together end-to-end and press the seam open. With *right* sides together sew the strip to the bottom edge of the sweatshirt, stopping at the curve (fig. 6). Trim off the excess. Tape under the remaining long edge (page 9). Press the strip to the wrong side of the sweatshirt and stitch in place along the taped edge.

Step 8 Center Front

For the center front, tape under one long edge of a 1½" x WOF strip. Sew the strip to the center front, *right* sides together, stopping at the curve (fig. 6). Let any extra length extend beyond the neck edge. Press the strip to the wrong side of the sweatshirt and stitch in place along the taped edge. Trim even with the neck edge. Repeat for the opposite center front.

Step 9 Facing the Curve

Tape along the wrong side of the inside curved edge of the facing pieces. Do not remove the paper from the tape. Clip the curves through but not beyond the edge of the tape. Press under the facing against the paper edge.

Remove the paper and stick the edge in place. Press under both ends of the facings ¼". With *right* sides together, sew the facings to the curved front edges of the sweatshirt, sewing past the hem and center front facing ends as shown (fig. 6). Clip the seam. Turn and press the facings to the wrong side and stitch in place along the taped edge. Hand stitch the small openings at the overlaps.

Step 10 Neck Edge

Press the 1½" x 40" bias strip in half, *wrong* sides together and matching the long raw edges. Sew to the right side of the neck edge, leaving at least ½" extending beyond each center front. Trim the ends to ½", tuck in, and press the strip to the wrong side. Stitch in place along the folded edge. Hand stitch the small openings at the center front closed.

Step 11 Sleeve Slits

Lay the sweatshirt face down on a flat surface, aligning the center fronts and smoothing the sleeves flat. With a fabric marker, mark a 4½" line at the center back of the sleeve, parallel with the top fold. Cut on the drawn line with scissors. Sew a button loop 1" from the sleeve edge as shown (fig. 7), leaving enough space in the loop for a 9/16" button. Repeat for the opposite sleeve.

Step 12 Finishing the Sleeve Slits

Press a 1½" x 12" bias strip in half, *wrong* sides together and matching raw edges. Sew the folded strip to the right side of the sleeve slit. Press to the wrong side and stitch in place. Trim off the excess length even with sleeve raw edge. Repeat for the opposite sleeve slit.

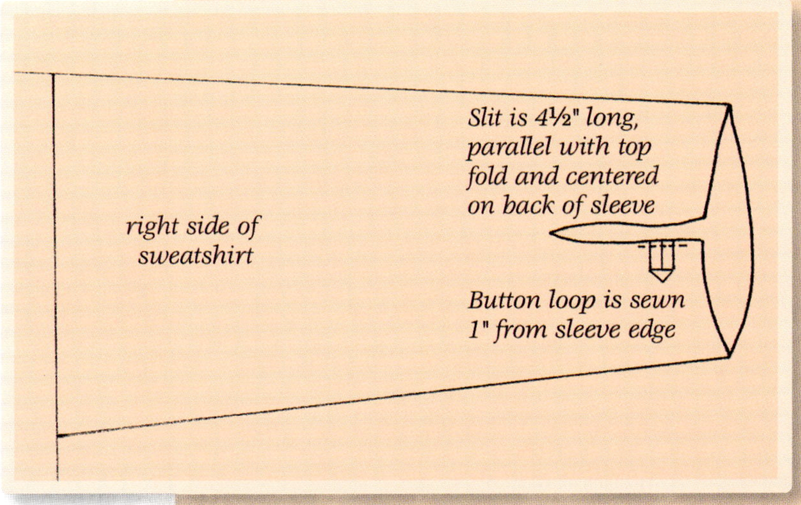

Fig. 7. Sleeve slit and botton loop

Step 13 Sleeve Cuff

Press a 1½" x WOF strip in half *wrong* sides together and matching raw edges. With *right* sides together, sew the strip to the sleeve edge, leaving ½" extending beyond the edges of the sleeve slit. Press the strip to the wrong side, tucking in the ends ½", and stitch in place along the folded edge. Hand stitch the small openings closed at the edges of the sleeve slit. Repeat for the opposite sleeve.

Step 14 Flower

Transfer eight flower patterns to the paper side of paper-backed fusible web. Cut out leaving a small margin around the drawn line. Fuse to the wrong side of the red fabric. Cut out on the drawn lines. Remove the paper and fuse two flowers on each center front above and below the waistband and on each side of the sleeve slits. Matching fabric and thread color, appliqué the edges of the flowers with a blanket stitch. With a fabric marker, transfer chenille lines to the sweatshirt and flowers.

Step 15 Chenille

Prepare Chenille By The Inch for application (pages 14–15). Using a ruler with ⅛" lines, trim chenille to ¼" wide (⅛" on each side of the stitched line). Sew the chenille to the sweatshirt and flowers following the transferred lines, back-tacking at the beginning and end of each strip to secure. Using a spray bottle with water, dampen the chenille strips. Brush vigorously to fluff using a Chenille Brush.

Sew the buttons at the sleeves and front.

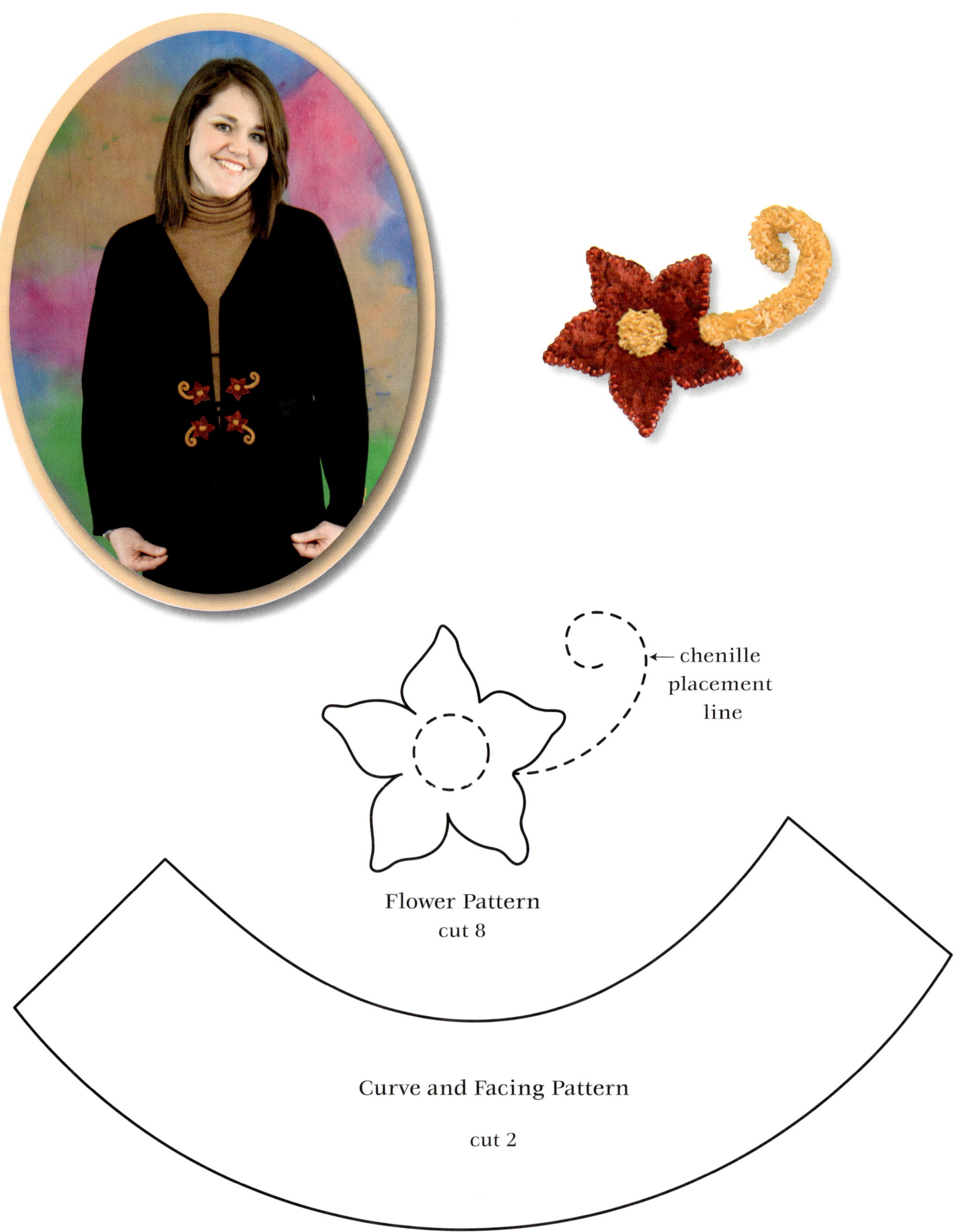
← chenille
placement
line
Flower Pattern
cut 8
Curve and Facing Pattern
cut 2

Drawstring Jacket

Drawstring Jacket

Materials

Pink sweatshirt
50" of Black Pepper Chenille By The Inch
Chenille Brush
Chenille Cutting Guide
Spray bottle with water
Long string to determine waist
Basic supplies as listed on page 9

Fabric Requirements and Cutting Instructions

* ⅓ yard pink mottled
  * One 1½" x 30" bias for neck (can be pieced)
  * Two 1½" x WOF for center fronts
  * Two 1½" x WOF for hem
  * One 1½" x WOF for sleeves
* ⅜ yard black
  * Two 2½" x WOF for waist drawstring casing
  * One 2½" x WOF for sleeve drawstring casings
  * Two 1¼" x WOF for waist drawstring
  * One 1¼" x WOF for sleeve drawstrings
* ⅛ yard woven, fusible interfacing
  * Three 1" x WOF strips

Making the Jacket

Step 1 Preparing the Sweatshirt

With scissors, cut off the bottom and sleeve bands from the sweatshirt. Remove the neckband with a seam ripper. Mark the center front of the sweatshirt and cut from the hem to the neck edge. Try on the sweatshirt and mark the hem and sleeve lengths ¼" *longer* than the desired finished length. Trim the hem and sleeves. (See Preparing the Sweatshirt, pages 10–13.)

Step 2 Hem

Fuse 1" x WOF interfacing to the wrong side of the sweatshirt ¼" above the bottom raw edge, overlapping ends to add another strip. Sew ½" x WOF pink hem facing together end-to-end and press the seam open. With *right* sides together, sew the strip to the bottom edge of the sweatshirt. Trim the excess even with the center front edges. Tape under the remaining long edge (page 9). Press the strip to the wrong side. Stitch in place along the taped edge.

Step 3 Center Front

Tape under one long edge of a 1½" x WOF strip. With *right* sides together and leaving at least ½" extending beyond the hem, sew the strip to the center front. Trim the hem end to ½". Press the strip to the wrong side, tucking in the end at the hem ½". Stitch in place along the taped edge. Hand stitch the small opening at the hem closed. Trim the other end even with the neck edge. Repeat for the opposite center front.

Step 4 Neck Edge

Press the 1½" x 30" bias strip in half, *wrong* sides together and matching the long raw edges. Sew to the neck edge, *right* sides together, leaving at least ½" extending beyond each center front. Trim the excess to ½", tuck in the ends, and press the strip to the wrong side. Stitch in place along the folded edge. Hand stitch the small openings at the center front closed.

Step 5 Sleeve Edge

Tape under one long edge of a 1½" x WOF strip, and press one end of the strip under ¼". With *right* sides together and starting with the pressed end, sew along the sleeve edge, overlapping the finishing end 1". Trim off the excess and press to the wrong side. Stitch in place along the taped edge. Hand stitch the small opening at the overlap closed. Repeat for the opposite sleeve using the remaining length of the strip.

Step 6 Tie Casing

Try on the sweatshirt and tie a string around your waist. Place a dot at each side at the string. This dot should be at your waist. (Mine fell 4" below the underarm seam.) Remove the sweatshirt, lay it flat, and draw a line around the sweatshirt at these dots (fig. 1, page 48).

Sew the 2½" x WOF drawstring casings end-to-end; press the seam open. Measure the distance around the entire sweatshirt on the drawn waistline. Trim the casing to this measurement plus 1". Fold under each end ¼", then another ¼"; press and stitch the folds in place. With *right* sides together and matching the long raw edges, sew to form a tube. Turn right side out and press the seam to the center back. Matching the top edge of the casing to the drawn line, topstitch in place along both edges of the casing, leaving the ends open (fig. 2).

Step 7 Drawstrings

Tape under both long edges of a 1" x WOF drawstring strip. Press the strip in half matching the folded edges and topstitch the folded edges together. Repeat for the sleeve drawstrings using the 1" x WOF sleeve drawstring strip. Cut in half and set aside for the sleeves. Thread the waist drawstring through the casing, trim to the desired length, and tie an overhand knot at each end.

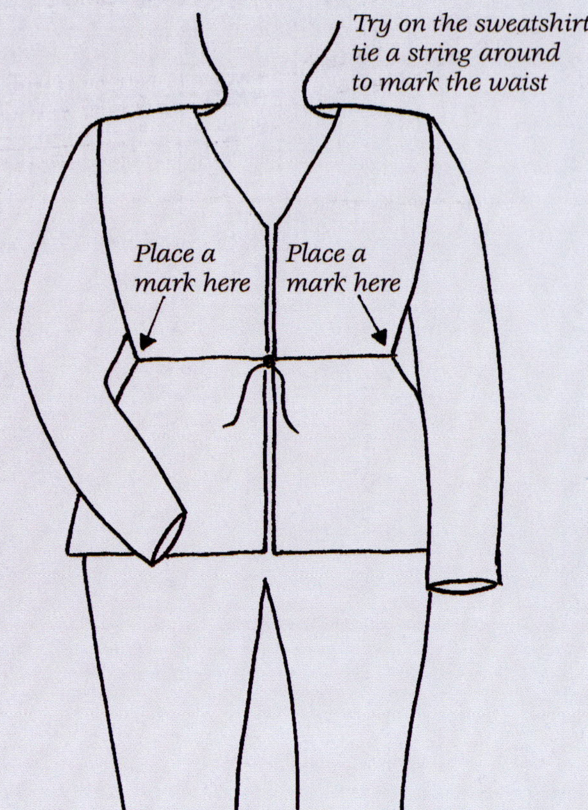

FIG. 1. Marking the waistband placement

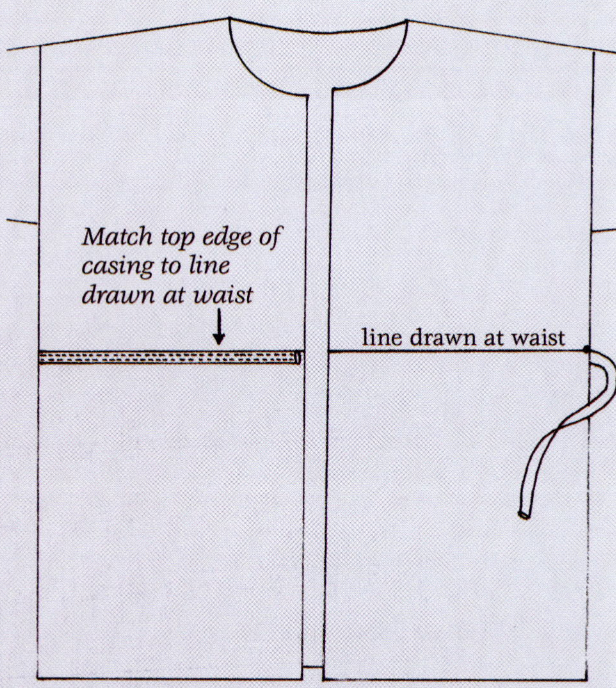

FIG. 2. Drawstring casing placement

Step 8 Sleeve Casing

Lay the sweatshirt flat and mark a 3" line parallel to the sleeve edge. Measure the distance around the sleeve at this line. Trim the 2½" x WOF sleeve casing strip to this length plus 1". Fold under each end ¼", then another ¼"; press and stitch the folds in place. With *right* sides together and matching the long raw edges, sew to form a tube. Turn right side out and press the seam to the center back. Matching the edge of the casing to the drawn line, topstitch in place along both edges of the casing, matching the ends and leaving an opening where the ends meet. Thread a sleeve drawstring through the casing, trim to the desired length, and tie an overhand knot in each end. Pull and tie the ends to the desired wrist width. Repeat for the opposite sleeve using the remaining lengths of casing strip and drawstring.

Step 9 Chenille

Prepare Chenille By The Inch for application as shown on pages 14–15. Sew chenille ½" from the neck edge, back-tacking at the beginning and end of each strip to secure and overlapping the ends to add a new strip. Using a spray bottle with water, dampen the sewn Chenille By The Inch strips. Brush vigorously with a Chenille Brush to fluff the chenille.

Round Neck Jacket

Round Neck Jacket

Materials

Navy sweatshirt

One 1¼" button

Two 1" buttons for pockets

Basic supplies as listed on page 9

Fabric Requirements and Cutting Instructions

- ½ yard black & pink print
  - One 1¾" x 30" bias for neck (can be pieced)
  - Two 1¾" x WOF for center fronts
  - One 1¾" x WOF for sleeves
  - One 1¾" x WOF for pocket trim
  - Two 4½" x 4½" squares for pocket lining
  - One button loop 1½" x 6" bias
- ¼" yard woven, fusible interfacing
  - Three 2" x WOF strips

Making the Jacket

Step 1 Preparing the Sweatshirt

With scissors, cut off the bottom and sleeve bands from the sweatshirt. Remove the neckband with a seam ripper. Mark the center front of the sweatshirt and cut from the hem to the neck edge. Try the sweatshirt on and mark the hem length 2½" *longer* than the desired finished length and the sleeve length ¼" *longer* than the desired length. Trim the hem and sleeves. (See Preparing the Sweatshirt, pages 10–13.)

Save the trimmed pieces for the pockets.

Step 2 Hem

Fuse the 2" x WOF strips of interfacing to the wrong side of the sweatshirt ½" from the bottom raw edge, overlapping the ends to add another strip. Press the hem under ½", then fold under another 2". Use wash-away tape to hold the hem in place (page 9). Stitch along the taped edge, then add another line of stitching to the hem ¼" below the first stitching line.

Step 3 Center Front

Tape under one long edge of a 1¾" x WOF strip. Sew the strip to the center front with the *right* side of the fabric to the *wrong* side of the sweatshirt, leaving at least ½" extending beyond the hem. Trim the ends to ½", tuck in the ends, and press the strip to the right side. Topstitch the strip in place along the taped edge. Hand stitch the small opening at the hem closed. Trim the other end even with the neck edge. Repeat for the opposite center front.

Step 4 Neck Edge

Tape under one long edge of the 1¾" x 30" bias strip. Sew the *right* side of the strip to the *wrong* side of the sweatshirt, leaving ½" extending beyond the center fronts. Trim the ends to ½", tuck in the ends, and press the strip to the right side. Topstitch along the taped edge. Hand stitch the small openings at the center front closed.

Step 5 Sleeve Cuff

Tape under one long edge of a 1¾" x WOF strip. Press one end of the strip under ¼". Sew the *right* side of the strip to the *wrong* side of the sleeve, starting with the pressed end and overlapping the finishing end 1". Trim off the excess. Press the seam toward the cuff. Fold the cuff to the right side along the seam and topstitch in place along the taped edge. Hand stitch the overlap closed. Repeat for the opposite cuff using the remaining length of the cuff strip.

Step 6 Pocket

Cut two pieces 4½" x 2½" from the trimmed hem or sleeve scraps. Sew the pieces together to make a 4½" x 4½" square. Press the seam open. Sew the pieced square to a 4½" x 4½" pocket lining, *right* sides together, leaving the top open and positioning the seam on the sweatshirt piece vertically. Clip the corners, turn right side out, and press. Sew the *right* side of a 1¾" x WOF strip to the *wrong* side of the open edge of the pocket edge, leaving ½" extending beyond each side. Trim the ends to ½". Tape under the fabric strip edge. Tuck in the ends, and press the strip along the seam to the right side of the pocket. Topstitch along the taped edge. Sew a 1" button at the center of the pocket trim. Repeat for the second pocket. Topstitch the pockets to the front of the jacket 2½" from the bottom edge and 2¾" from the center front edge, leaving the top open.

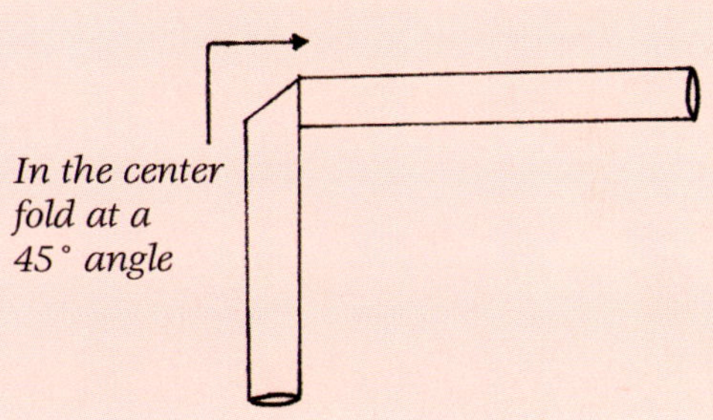

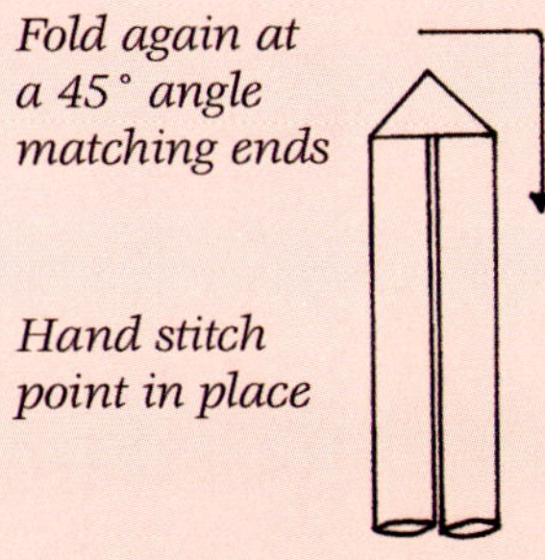

Fig. 1. Making button loops

Step 7 Button Loop

Fold a 1½" x 6" bias strip in half, *right* sides together and matching the long raw edges. Sew, forming a tube. Turn right side out. Press the seam to the center back. Fold as shown and press (fig. 1). Hand stitch the folds in place. Press under the raw ends and sew the loop to the right front (as you're wearing the jacket) of the neck edge, leaving enough room for a 1¼" button. Sew the button to the opposite center front.

Long Tunic

Long Tunic

Materials

Black sweatshirt

Five 1" buttons

150" of Peanut Butter Cup Chenille By The Inch

Chenille Brush

Chenille Cutting Guide

Spray bottle with water

Basic supplies as listed on page 9

Fabric Requirements and Cutting Instructions

- 2½ yards black
  - Four 14½" x WOF for bottom and bottom lining
  - Two 3½" x WOF for center front plackets
  - Two 4½" x 30" for collar and collar lining
  - Two 4½" x 20½" for cuffs

- 2¼ yards woven, fusible interfacing
  - Four 14" x WOF for bottom and bottom lining
  - Two 3" x WOF for center front plackets
  - One 4" x WOF for collar and collar lining
  - Two 4" x 20" for cuffs

Making the Jacket

Step 1 Preparing the Sweatshirt

With scissors, cut off the bottom and sleeve bands from the sweatshirt. Do not remove the neck band. Mark the center front of the sweatshirt and cut from the hem to the neck edge. Try on the sweatshirt and mark the hem length 14" *shorter* than the desired finished length. Mark the sleeve length ¼" *longer* than the desired length. Trim the hem and sleeves. (See Preparing the Sweatshirt, pages 10–13.)

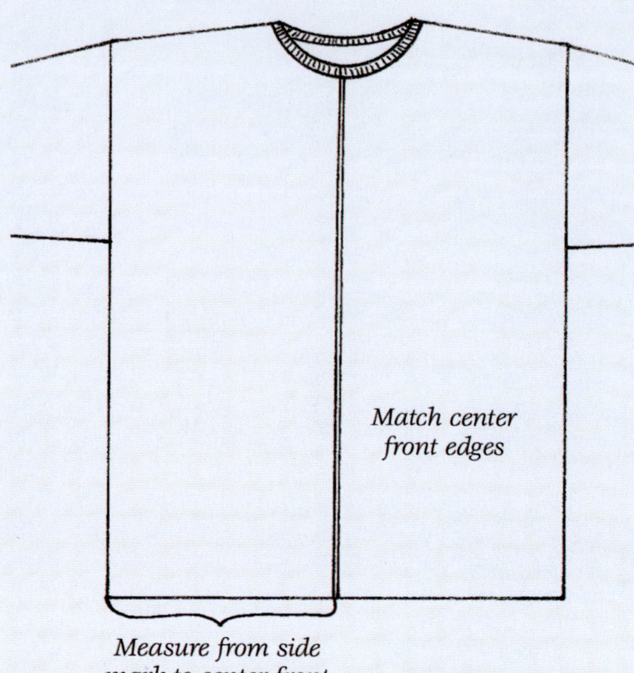

Fig. 1. Measuring the bottom

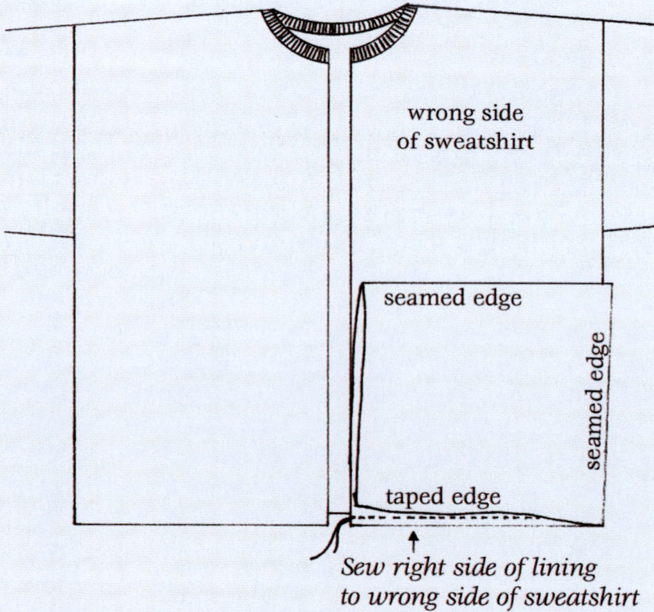

Fig. 2. Adding the lining to the sweatshirt

Step 2 Center Front Extensions

Lay the sweatshirt flat, butting the center fronts. Draw a mark at the side folds. Measure the bottom raw edge of the sweatshirt front from the side mark to the center front opening (fig. 1).

Add ¼" to the front measurement and cut two sections (for the extension and lining) from the 14½" x WOF strips equal to this measurement. Cut two pieces of interfacing ¼" smaller on all sides. Center and fuse the interfacing to the wrong side of each section. Sew the pieces together along two adjacent sides, *right* sides together. Clip the corner, turn, and press. Tape under the long edge of the outer section (page 9). Sew the *right* side of the lining to the *wrong* side of the sweatshirt, matching the raw edges and the center front (fig. 2). Press the seam toward the lining.

Match the taped edge of the outer fabric to the stitching line and topstitch in place (fig. 3). Repeat for the opposite center front.

Step 3 Back Extensions

Measure the back raw edge between the side marks; add ½" to this measurement. Cut two sections (for the back extension and lining) from the remaining 14½" x WOF strips to equal this measurement. Cut two pieces of interfacing ¼" smaller on all sides. Center and fuse the interfacing to the wrong side of each section. Sew the sections along three sides, *right* sides together, leaving one long side open. Clip the corners, turn, and press. Tape under the long edge of the extension. Sew the *right* side of the lining to the *wrong* side of the sweatshirt, matching the raw edges and the sides. Press the seam toward the lining. Topstitch the extension in place, matching the taped edge to the first stitching line.

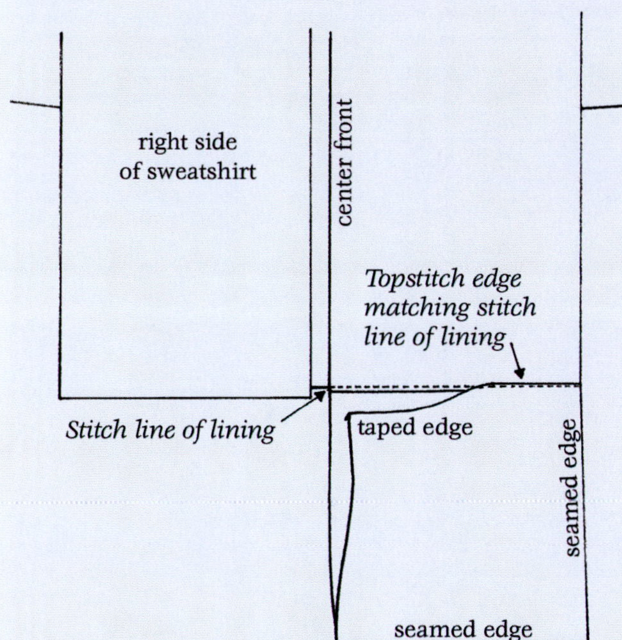

Fig. 3. Topstitch lining in place

Step 4 Back Box Pleat

Fold the sweatshirt in half, matching the shoulder and underarm seams. Draw a line at the back center fold. Draw a line 1" from each side of the center line. Draw another line 4" above the extension seam (fig. 4). Fold the sweatshirt on the outer lines and bring the folds in to the center line, forming a box pleat. Use wash-away tape to hold the pleat in place between the 4" line and the extension seam. Press. Topstitch the pleat ½" from the center folded edges and across the top and bottom of the pleat. Add a small triangle of stitching just below the extension seam to hold the shape of the pleat in the back extension.

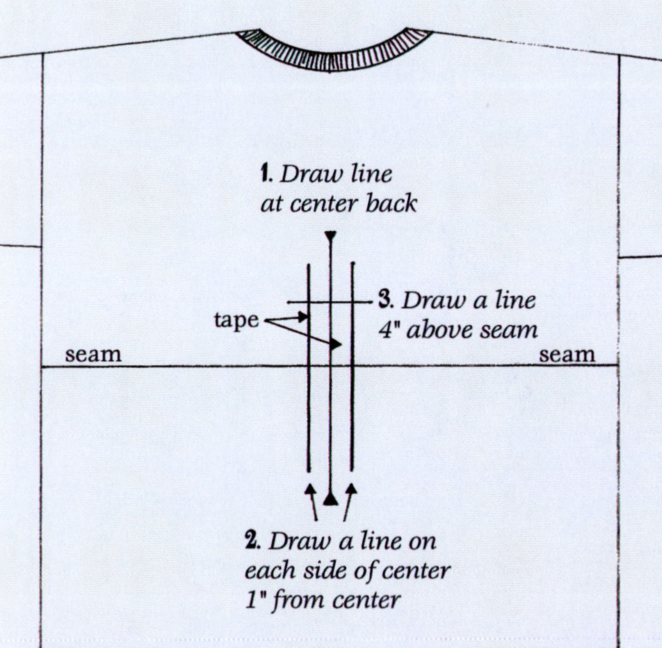

Fig. 4. Back box pleat

Step 5 Center Front Placket

Center a 3" x WOF strip of interfacing on the wrong side of a 3½" x WOF front placket strip and fuse in place. Sew the *right* side of the placket to the *wrong* side of the center front edge, leaving ½" extending beyond the hem and ¼" extending beyond the neck band. Tape under the remaining long edge of the placket. Trim the placket ends at the hem to ½", tuck in the ends, and press the placket to the right side of the sweatshirt, matching the taped edge with the stitching line (fig. 5, page 58). (The center front placket should be ¼" shorter than the neck band edge.) Topstitch in place along the taped edge. Hand stitch small openings at the hem and neck closed. Repeat for the opposite center front.

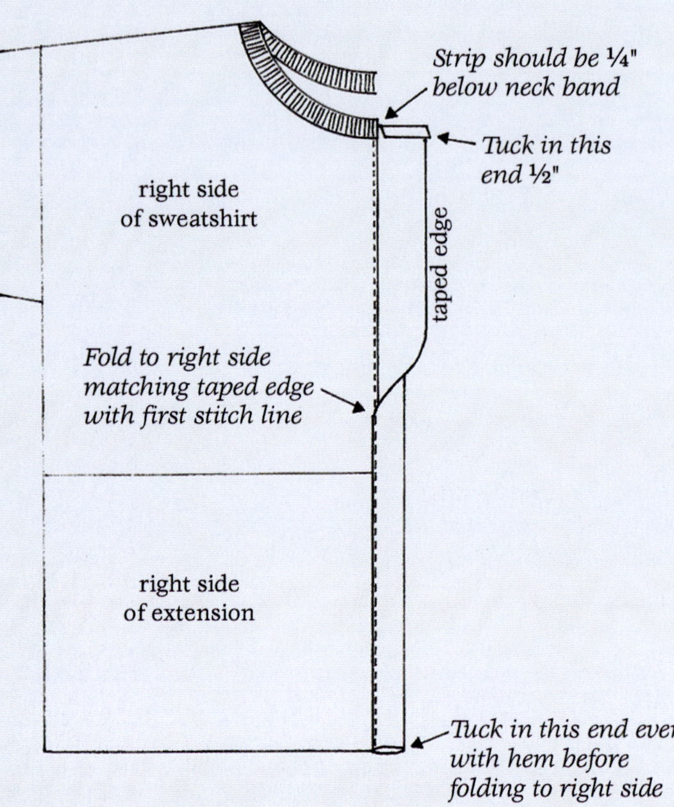

FIG. 5. Center front placket

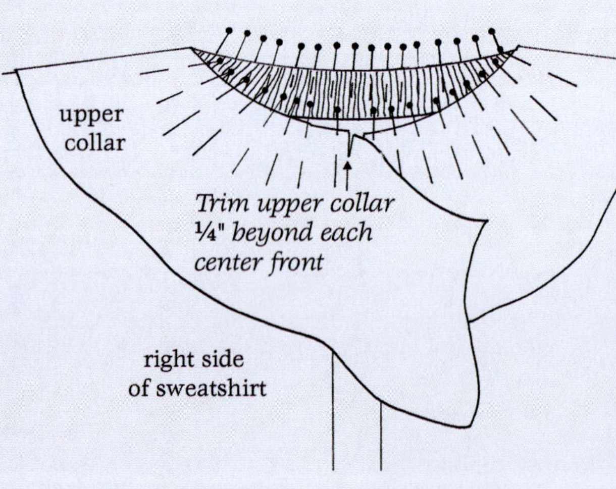

FIG. 6. Pin collar to neckband

Step 6 Making the Collar

Pin the collar piece to the neckband, starting at the center front and extending ¼" beyond each center front (fig. 6). Trim the excess.

Remove the collar from the neckband. Trim the 4½" x 30" collar lining to match the collar piece. Cut two pieces from the 4" x WOF interfacing ½" smaller than the collar. Center and fuse the interfacing to the wrong sides of the collar and lining. Tape under one long edge of the collar. Sew the collar and lining on three sides, *right* sides together, leaving the side with the taped edge open. Trim the corners, turn right side out, and press.

Step 7 Adding the Collar

Sew the collar lining to the neckband, *right* sides together, matching the side collar seams to the center front edges of the neckband (fig. 7). Press the seam toward the lining. Pin the taped edge of the collar to the neckband, matching the stitching line. Topstitch in place along the taped edge. Put the jacket on to help determine the proper collar fold, then press.

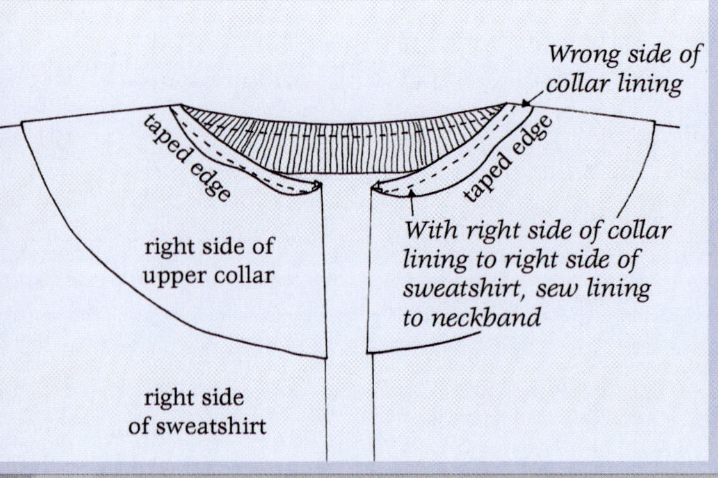

FIG. 7. Sew collar lining to neckband

Step 8 Sleeve Cuff

Center and fuse a 4" x 20" interfacing to the wrong side of a 4½" x 20½" cuff. Tape under one long edge of the cuff. Press one end of the cuff under ¼". Sew the cuff to the sleeve edge, *right* sides together, starting with the pressed end and overlapping the finishing end 1". Trim off the excess. Press the seam toward the cuff. Fold the cuff under and stitch in place, matching the taped edge with the stitching line. Hand stitch the overlap closed. Repeat for the opposite cuff using the remaining length of the cuff strip.

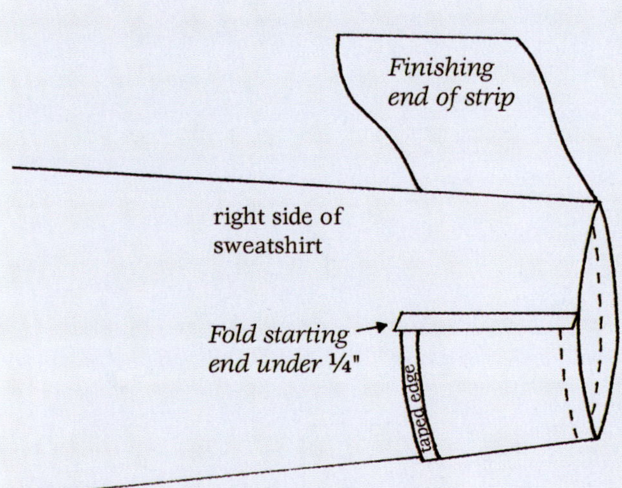

Fig. 7. Sleeve cuff

Step 9 Chenille

Prepare Chenille By The Inch for application (pages 14–15). Sew chenille to the collar and cuffs ½" from the edge. Sew chenille along the center front placket seams. Back-tack at the beginning and end of each strip to secure and overlap the ends to add a new strip. Dampen the sewn chenille strips with a spray bottle of water and brush vigorously with a Chenille Brush to fluff the chenille.

Step 10 Buttonholes

Mark placement for 5 buttonholes on the right (as you're wearing the tunic) center front. Make the buttonholes and sew the buttons on the opposite placket.

Flower Medallion Jacket

Flower Medallion Jacket

Materials

Black sweatshirt

1 yard lightweight, paper-backed fusible web

Small amount of pattern tracing material (or tissue paper)

Black hook and eye

Basic supplies as listed on page 9

Fabric Requirements and Cutting Instructions

- ⅝ yard bright paisley print
  - One 1½" x 40" bias for neck (can be pieced)
  - Two 1½" x WOF for center fronts
  - Two 1½" x WOF for hem
  - One 1½" x WOF for sleeves
  - Three 11" x 11" squares for appliqué
- ⅓ yard white
  - Three flower patterns from pattern

Making the Jacket

Step 1 Preparing the Sweatshirt

With scissors, cut off the bottom and sleeve bands from the sweatshirt. Remove the neckband with a seam ripper. Mark the center front of the sweatshirt and cut from the hem to the neck edge. Try on the sweatshirt and mark the hem and sleeve lengths ¼" *longer* than the desired finished length. Trim the hem and sleeves. (See Preparing the Sweatshirt, pages 10–13.)

Step 2 Making the Flowers

Trace three flower patterns (page 64) onto the paper side of paper-backed fusible web, mirror imaging the second half to create the full flower. Cut out beyond the outside drawn line, leaving about a ¼" margin around each flower. Fuse to the *wrong* side of the white fabric. Cut out exactly on the inside and outside lines. Remove the paper backing. Cut three 11" x 11" squares of paper-backed fusible web. Fuse to the *wrong* side of 11" x 11" squares of paisley print. Do not remove the paper backing. Fuse the white flowers to the center of the paisley print squares. Cut out exactly on the outer lines of the white flowers. Remove the paper backing.

Step 3 Fuse Flowers

Referring to the photos, fuse one flower to the lower right (as you're wearing the jacket) center front and hem, allowing some of the flower to extend beyond the edges. Fuse the second flower to the left neck edge and the third to the right back shoulder, allowing a portion of both flowers to extend beyond the neck edge. With scissors, trim the flowers even with the sweatshirt. Appliqué both the inner and outer edges of the flowers with white thread and a blanket stitch.

Step 4 Hem

Press a 1½" x WOF paisley print strip in half, *wrong* sides together and matching the long raw edges. Sew the strip to the right side of the hem edge and press to the wrong side. Stitch in place along the folded edge, switching to white thread at the flower.

Step 5 Center Front

Press a 1½" x WOF paisley print strip in half, *wrong* sides together and matching the long raw edges. Sew the strip to the right side of the center front, leaving ½" extending beyond the hem. Press the strip to the wrong side, tucking in the end at the hem ½" and trimming the other end even with the neck edge. Stitch the strip in place along the folded edge. Hand stitch the opening at the hem closed. Repeat for the opposite center front edge.

Step 6 Neck Edge

Press the 1½" x 40" paisley print bias strip in half, *wrong* sides together and matching the long raw edges. Sew the strip to the right side of the neck edge, leaving an extra ½" extending beyond each center front. Trim the ends to ½", tuck in the ends, and press the strip to the wrong side. Stitch in place, switching to white thread at the flowers. Hand stitch the center front openings closed.

Step 7 Sleeve

Press a 1½" x WOF paisley print strip in half, *wrong* sides together and matching the long raw edges. Fold under one end of the strip ¼" and press. Sew the *right* side of the strip to the *right* side of the sleeve, starting with the pressed end and overlapping the finishing end 1". Trim off the excess. Press the strip to the wrong side and stitch in place. Hand stitch the small overlap closed. Repeat for the other sleeve using the remaining length of the strip.

Option

If you'd like the trim to show at the sleeve hem, sew the strip to the wrong side first, turn to the outside, and topstitch in place.

Step 8 Fastening

Hand sew a hook and eye at the neck edge.

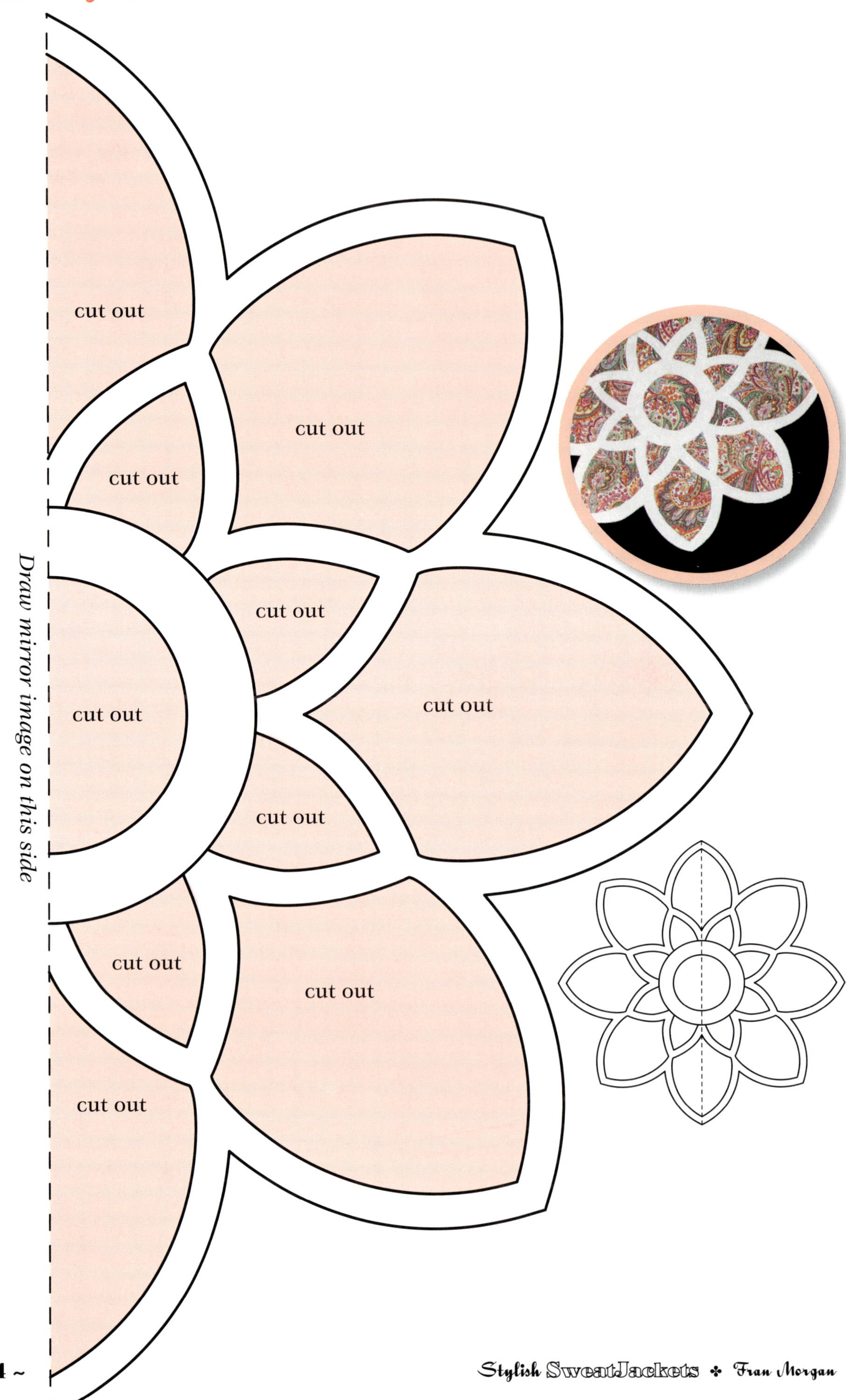
cut out
cut out
cut out
cut out
cut out
cut out
cut out
cut out
cut out
cut out
Draw mirror image on this side

Ruffled Jacket

Ruffled Jacket

Materials

Navy sweatshirt

Seven ⅝" buttons

Ruffling presser foot (optional)

Basic supplies as listed on page 9

Fabric Requirements and Cutting Instructions

- ⅔ yard beige polka dot
  - One 1½" x 40" bias strip for neck
  - Two 1½" x WOF for hem
  - Two 2½" x WOF for center fronts
  - One 1" x WOF for sleeve edge
  - Five 1½" x WOF for ruffles
- ⅜ yard woven, fusible interfacing
  - Three 1" x WOF for hem
  - Four 2" x WOF for center fronts

Making the Jacket

Step 1 Preparing the Sweatshirt

With scissors, cut off the bottom and sleeve bands from the sweatshirt. Remove the neckband with a seam ripper. Mark the center front of the sweatshirt and cut from the hem to the neck edge. Try on the sweatshirt and mark the hem length ¼" *longer* than the desired finished length and sleeve length ½" *shorter* than the desired finished length. Trim the hem and sleeves. (See Preparing the Sweatshirt pages 10–13.)

Mark and cut a V-neck (fig. 1).

Step 2 Hem

Fuse the 1" x WOF interfacing to the *wrong* side of the sweatshirt ¼" from the bottom raw edge, overlapping the ends to add another strip. Sew two 1½" x WOF strips together end-to-end; press the seam open. Tape under one long edge of the strip (page 9). With *right* sides together, sew the strip to the bottom edge; press the strip to the wrong side. Stitch the strip along the taped edge. Trim the ends even with the center front edges.

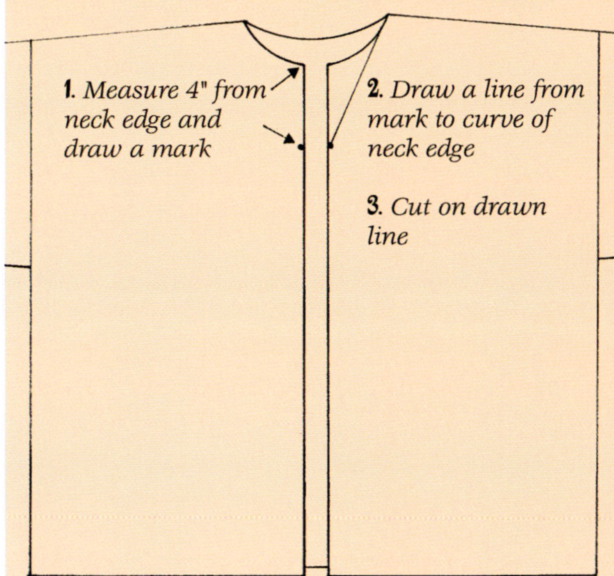

FIG. 1. Marking V-neck

Step 3 Center Front

Center and press one 2" x WOF interfacing strip to the *wrong* side of a 2½" x WOF polka dot strip. Tape under one long edge. Sew the *right* side of the strip to the *wrong* side of the sweatshirt center front, leaving ½" extending beyond the hem. Press the strip to the right side and fold in half, matching the taped edge to the stitching line and tucking in the ½" at the end. Pin in place. Trim the other end along the neck edge. Repeat for the opposite center front (fig. 2).

Step 4 Neck Edge

Tape under one long edge of the polka dot 1½" x 40" bias strip. Sew the *right* side of the bias strip to the *wrong* side of the neck edge, leaving at least ½" extending beyond the center front. Press to the right side and trim the ends to ½". Tuck in the ends at each center front and pin in place. (fig. 2)

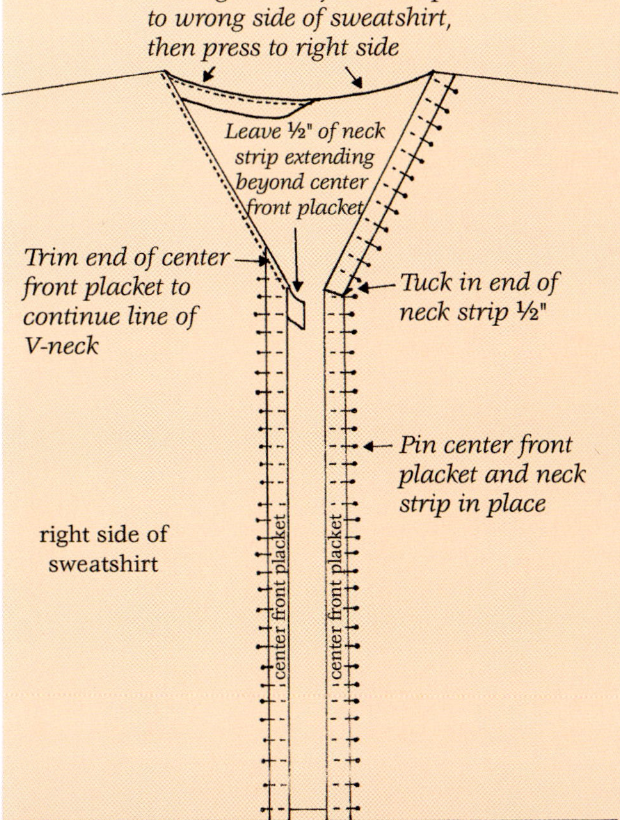

FIG. 2. Neck edge

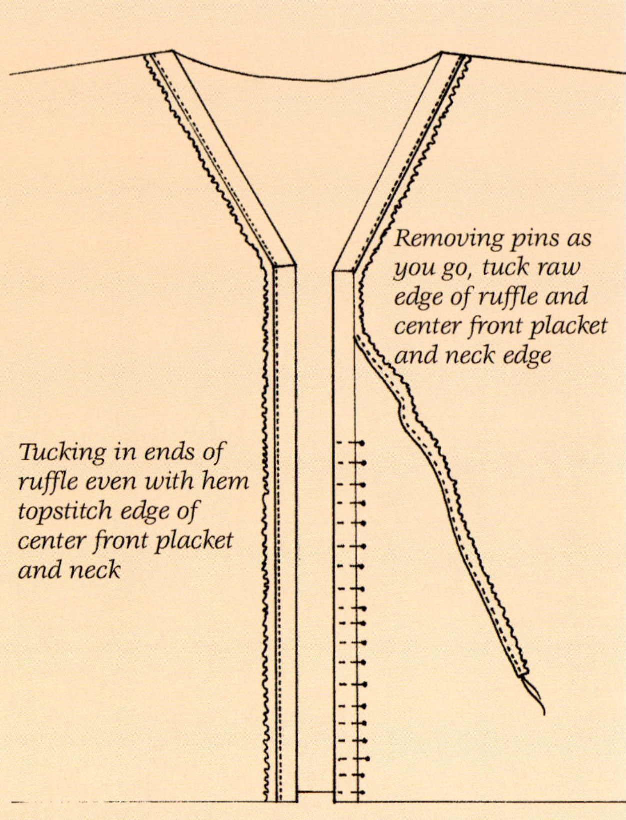

FIG. 3. Neck edge ruffle

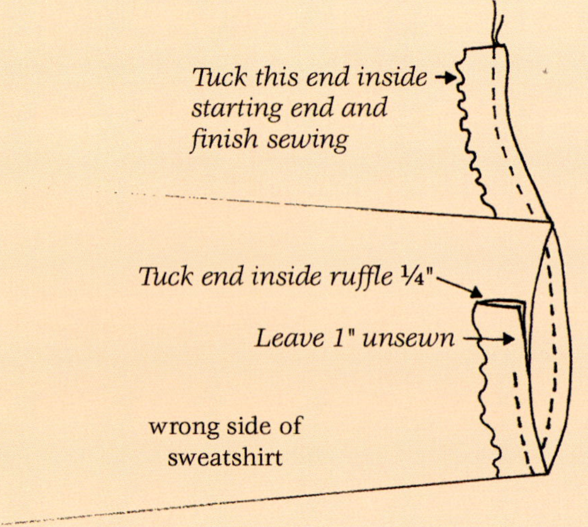

FIG. 4. Sleeve edge ruffle

Step 5 Ruffle

Sew five 1½" x WOF strips together end-to-end; press the seams open. Fold the strip in half, *wrong* sides together and matching the long raw edges, and press. Using a ruffling foot or the method of your choice, gather the raw edges of the folded strip, sewing through both thicknesses.

Starting at a center front hem edge and leaving ½" extending beyond the hem, tape the raw edge of the ruffle under the center front and neck trim, removing pins as you go (fig. 3). Trim the excess and set aside for the sleeves. Tuck the ends inside the ruffle even with the hem and press. Topstitch the center fronts and neck edges along the taped edge, sewing through all thicknesses. Hand stitch the small openings at the hem closed. Hand stitch the opening where the neck trim and center fronts overlap.

Step 6 Sleeve Edge Ruffle

Sew the ruffle to the *wrong* side of the sleeve edge, tucking in the end ½" and leaving 1" unsewn at the beginning. Tuck the finishing end inside the starting end, stitch in place, and trim off the excess (fig. 4).

With wash-away tape, tape under one long edge of a 1" x WOF strip. Press under one end ¼". Starting with the pressed end, sew the *right* side of the strip to the *wrong* side of the sleeve, sandwiching the ruffle, and overlapping the finishing end ½" (fig. 5). Trim off the excess and set aside for the second sleeve. Press the strip and ruffle to the right side of the sweatshirt.

Topstitch the edge of the strip in place. Hand stitch the overlap closed. Repeat for the opposite sleeve using the remaining lengths of ruffle and 1" strip.

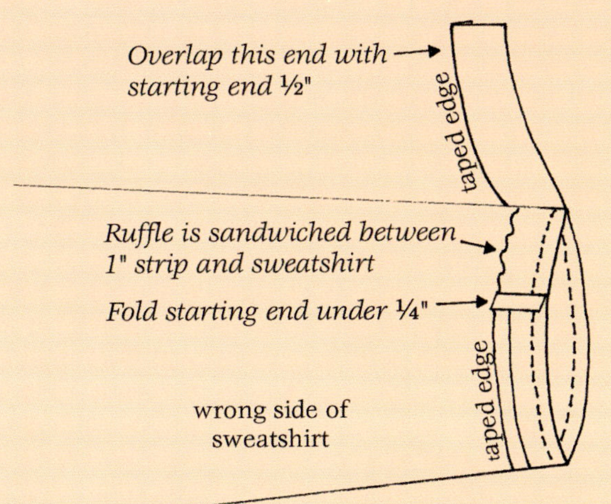

Fig. 5. Sleeve trim

Step 7 Buttonholes & Buttons

Mark buttonhole placement for 7 buttons in the center of the right (as you're wearing the jacket) placket. Make the buttonholes and sew the buttons on the opposite placket.

Poinsettia Jacket

Poinsettia Jacket

Materials

Black sweatshirt

12 gold 9 mm jingle bells

¼ yard lightweight, paper-backed fusible web

Black hook and eye

Ruffling presser foot (optional)

Basic supplies as listed on page 9

Fabric Requirements and Cutting Instructions

- ⅝ yard black and gold stripe
  - Three 1½" x WOF for center front facing and cuffs
  - Two 1" x WOF for bottom ruffle trim
  - One 1" x 35" bias for neck edge
  - Two 4½" x WOF for ruffle
- ¼ yard red swirl fabric
  - Three large poinsettias from pattern
- ⅛ yard green swirl fabric
  - Three small poinsettias from pattern

Making the Jacket

Step 1 Preparing the Sweatshirt

With scissors, cut off the bottom and sleeve bands from the sweatshirt. Do not remove the neck band. Mark the center front of the sweatshirt and cut from the hem to the neck edge. Try on the sweatshirt and mark the hem length 2" *shorter* than the desired finished length and the sleeve length ¼" *longer* than the desired finished length. Trim the hem and sleeves. (See Preparing the Sweatshirt, pages 10–13.)

Step 2 Center Front

Press a 1½" x WOF strip in half, *wrong* sides together and matching the long raw edges. Sew the strip to the *wrong* side of the center front, positioning one end of the strip ½" from the top edge of the neckband, letting the excess fall beyond the bottom edge. Press the strip to the right side and topstitch in place. Trim the excess even with the bottom edge. Repeat for the opposite center front.

Step 3 Hem Ruffle

Sew two 4½" x WOF strips together end-to-end; press the seam open. Press the strip in half, *wrong* sides together and matching the long raw edges. Using a ruffling foot or method of your choice, gather the raw edges of the folded strip, sewing through both thicknesses. Tape the ruffle to the *wrong* side of the sweatshirt using water-soluble basting tape (page 9), leaving ½" extending beyond the center front edges. Tuck in the ½" ends of the ruffle to match the center front edges.

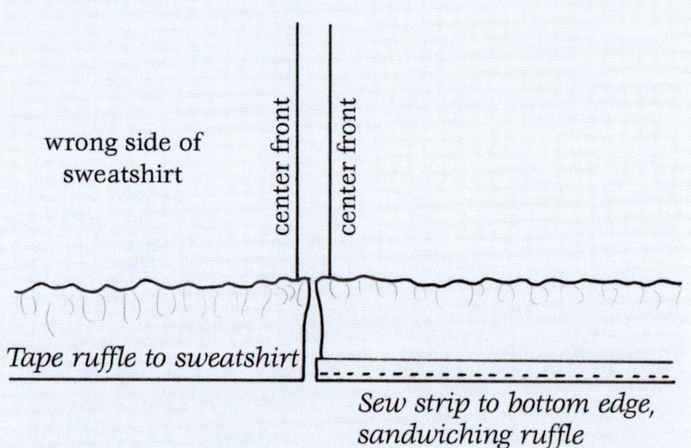

Fig. 1. Adding ruffle to sweatshirt

Press a 1" x WOF strip of black and gold stripe in half, *wrong* sides together and matching the long raw edges. Sew the strip to the bottom raw edge of the sweatshirt, sandwiching the ruffle between the strip and the sweatshirt, leaving at least ½" extending beyond the center front edge (fig. 1). Press the strip to the front and press the ruffle away from the sweatshirt. Trim to ½". Tuck in the ½" ends and topstitch along the folded edge of the strip. Hand sew the small openings at the center front of the strip and ruffle closed.

Step 4 Neck

Press the 1½" x 35" bias strip in half, *wrong* sides together and matching the long raw edges. Tape the raw edge along the manufacturer's stitching line for the neckband, leaving ½" extending beyond the center front edges. Trim the excess. Tuck under edges ½" to match the center front edges. Fold the sweatshirt neckband over, covering the raw edge of the bias strip, and tape in place. Tuck in the ends of the neckband to match the center front. Topstitch the edge of the neckband to secure the top edge of the bias strip. Topstitch the folded edge of the bias strip to the sweatshirt. Hand stitch the small openings at the center fronts closed.

Step 5 Sleeve

Press a 1½" x WOF strip in half, *wrong* sides together and matching the long raw edges. Fold under one end of the strip ¼" and press. Sew the *right* side of the strip to the *wrong* side of the sleeve, starting with the pressed end and overlapping the finishing end 1". Trim off the excess. Press the strip to the right side and topstitch in place. Hand stitch the overlap closed. Repeat for the other sleeve using the remaining length of the strip.

Step 6 Poinsettias

Trace three large poinsettias and three small poinsettia patterns (page 74) onto the paper side of the paper-backed fusible web. Cut out, leaving a small margin around the drawn line. Fuse the large poinsettias to the wrong side of the red fabric and small poinsettias to the wrong side of the green fabric. Cut out on the drawn lines. Remove the paper and fuse one large poinsettia to the left (as you're wearing it) front shoulder and two large poinsettias to the right back shoulder. Appliqué in place with red thread and a blanket stitch. Fuse one small poinsettia in the center of each large poinsettia. Appliqué in place with green thread and a blanket stitch. Hand sew three jingle bells to the center of each small poinsettia.

Step 7 Fastening

Sew a hook and eye to the center front at the neck edge.

Small
Poinsettia
Large
Poinsettia

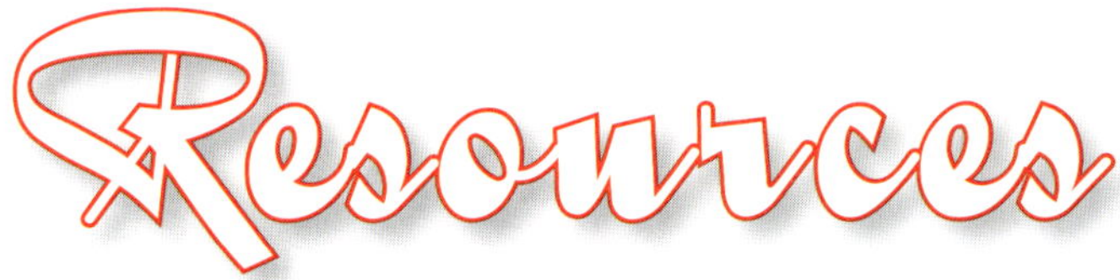

Resources

Before contacting the resource companies, please check with your local quilt shop for their fabulous fabric selections and tools.

For sweatshirts, Chenille By The Inch®, the Chenille Brush™, the Chenille Cutting Guide™, interfacing, water-soluble basting tape, fabric markers, and other tools:

Fabric Café
Toll Free 866-855-0998
www.fabriccafe.com

For zippers and organza:
Ghee's
318-226-1701
www.ghees.com

Meet the Author

Fran Morgan leads the design efforts and is a co-owner of Fabric Café®. A designer and author for over 18 years, Fran has appeared on television programs including *Simply Quilts, America Sews, Quilting with Shar, Sew Much More, Kaye Wood Quilting Friends,* and *American Quilter.*

With well over 100 patterns and books with her byline, Fran has been published under the company names of the American Quilter's Society, Dynamic Resource Group, as well as Fabric Café. She designs using varied techniques including quilting, structural fabric forms, needlepoint, and crochet. Fabric Café frequently ships Fran's patterns and books around the world. To see the versatility of this fiber artist, visit her Web site at **www.fabriccafe.com**.